DIGITAL MUSIC

COMPUTERS THAT MAKE MUSIC

01000010110
11000011100
10110001011
11011011010
00110010100
00011000011
01000010110
11000011100
10110001011
11011011010
00110010100
00011000011
01000010110
11000011100
10110001011
11011011010

THE DIGITAL WORLD

THE DIGITAL WORLD

DIGITAL MUSIC
COMPUTERS THAT MAKE MUSIC

ANANDA MITRA, PH.D.

CHELSEA HOUSE
PUBLISHERS
An imprint of Infobase Publishing

DIGITAL MUSIC: Computers That Make Music

Chelsea House
An imprint of Infobase Publishing
132 West 31st Street
New York NY 10001

Library of Congress Cataloging-in-Publication Data
Mitra, Ananda, 1960–
    Digital music : computers that make music / Ananda Mitra.
        p. cm. — (The digital world)
    Includes bibliographical references and index.
    ISBN 978-0-8160-6787-9 (hardcover)
    1. Digital music players—Juvenile literature.   2. Digital jukebox software—Juvenile literature.
3. Music and the Internet—Juvenile literature.   4. Copyright—Sound recordings—Juvenile
literature.   I. Title.   II. Series.

    ML74.M58 2010
    786.7'6—dc22

                                                                            2009052509

Text design by Annie O'Donnell
Cover design by Takeshi Takahashi
Composition by Newgen
Cover printed by Yurchak Printing, Landisville, Pa.
Book printed and bound by Yurchak Printing, Landisville, Pa.
Printed in the United States of America

This book is printed on acid-free paper.

All links and Web addresses were checked and verified to be correct at the time of publication. Because of the dynamic nature of the Web, some addresses and links may have changed since publication and may no longer be valid.

Contents

Preface

These days, it is not unusual for 10- to 12-year-olds to be publishing their own Web sites or for second and third graders to begin computer classes. At the same time, computer games are becoming increasingly popular as major publishing houses continue to churn out educational computer programs for children in preschool. At the other end of the spectrum, technological know-how has become a requirement for most jobs in an increasingly digital world, as the computer has become a common tool in most professions. Even the often-mentioned "digital divide" between those who have access to computers and those who do not is being bridged with the development of tools such as the XD computer designed by the Massachusetts Institute of Technology Media Laboratory and the availability of computers at libraries and schools. As people become more reliant on digital devices to perform everyday tasks, these modern conveniences become commonplace.

Even though there are many different kinds of computers available for everyday use—ranging from gadgets like the BlackBerry to specially made computers for playing computer games—all the machines operate on the fundamental system of ones and zeros called binary, invented in the seventeenth century. Although it might appear that computers and newly developed digital products are "new" technologies, the seeds of modern digital technologies were planted nearly three centuries ago and grew with the research of legendary scholars and engineers such as Gottfried Leibniz and others.

The relevance of digital technologies in everyday life often has been overshadowed by market-driven hype about new technologies that appear to be introduced at a breakneck speed, which leaves so many people scrambling to catch up to the latest gadget. This result, however, is the surface representation of deeper changes in society that are taking place with the adoption of digital tools in different aspects of everyday life. THE DIGITAL WORLD is a set of volumes that aims to explore the whole spectrum of applications, describing how digital systems influence society and helping readers understand the nature of digital systems and their many interacting parts. The set covers major applications of digital systems and includes the following titles:

- *Digital Communications*
- *Digital Games*
- *Digital Music*
- *Digital Research*
- *Digital Security*
- *Digital Video*

Each volume in the set explores a wide range of material, explains the basic concepts of these applications, and then discusses the implications they have on everyday life. Because the number of possible topics is practically limitless, we focus on a sample of the most interesting and useful applications and tools and explain the basic principles of technology. Readers are encouraged to continue exploring the digital world with the guidance of our Further Resources section featured in each volume. The goal of these books is to encourage the reader to see the relevance of digital systems in all aspects of life, at the present time as well as in the past and in the years to come.

Acknowledgments

I would like to thank a group of people who made this book possible. My thanks first goes to my family in America and India who provided support and balance to my writing life. Appreciation also goes to my friends in Winston-Salem and colleagues at Wake Forest University who provided the encouragement throughout the entire process of doing the six books in this series. Thanks also goes to Elizabeth Oakes for providing photographs that illustrate the different components of the digital world and to Jodie Rhodes, who helped me overcome more than one challenge. Finally, I thank the editors for their patience and encouragement to ensure we create a worthy product. General thanks goes to the publisher for giving me this opportunity.

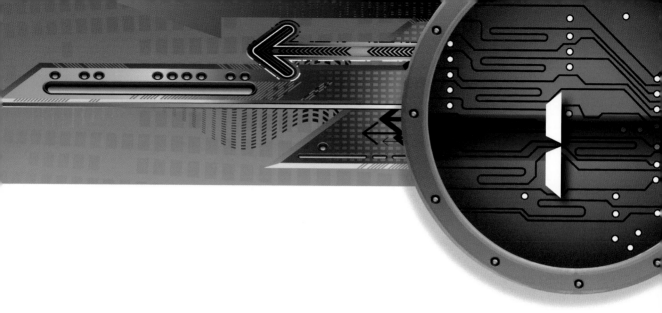

Basics of Sound

Digital music makes up one of the most important parts of the digital world. Compact discs (CDs), digital music players like iPods, Internet radio stations, and podcasts are used by millions of people. In fact, the iPod has become one of the most popular electronic gadgets, seen everywhere from airports to school classrooms. All age groups, from the very young to the elderly, use CD players to listen to digital music. Seeing people with earphones listening to digital music has become a common sight. Digital sound is also used in home appliances, such as talking toasters, and for sending voice commands on the telephone. Listening to digital sound is the first step toward appreciating its complex world. The next step is gaining information.

Sound is made up of traveling vibrations, just like waves that travel across still water when the water is disturbed. When a pebble falls into a still pond, it creates waves that move outward from the place where the pebble fell into the water. The waves are large at the

Musical Notes

1 Waveform

2 Waveform of 440 Hz note

Violin

Displacement / Time

Piano

Displacement / Time

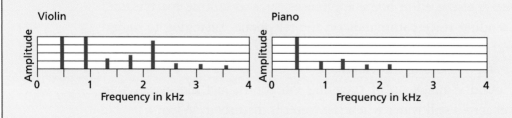

3 Frequency spectrum of 440 Hz note

Violin

Amplitude / Frequency in kHz

Piano

Amplitude / Frequency in kHz

point where the pebble is dropped and become smaller as they move out from that spot, until they eventually disappear.

Sound behaves in a similar fashion. As the *Columbia Encyclopedia on Physics* explains, "When a body vibrates, or moves back and forth, the oscillation [back-and-forth movement] causes a periodic disturbance of the surrounding air or other medium that radiates outward in straight lines in the form of a pressure wave. The effect these waves produce upon the ear is perceived as sound." Vibrations produced by gadgets such as a loudspeaker produce sound waves similar to the waves in water. Loudspeaker vibrations cause pressure differences in the surrounding air as they travel. These pressure differences cause sound sensors such as the eardrum to vibrate, which is interpreted by the brain as the sound produced by the loudspeaker. Sound only exists when there are vibrations in a medium such as air, and sound can be heard only when there is something to detect the vibrations.

This chapter describes the way in which sound vibrations are changed into digital information that can be manipulated by computers. We will also look at the process of digitization that makes sound waves into digital files, which can then be treated in the same way as any other digital data.

HOW SOUND IS PRODUCED

Sound can be produced by any system that is capable of causing vibrations in a medium. For example, there are natural sources of sound wherein the vibrations are produced without any human involvement, such as leaves that rustle when wind blows through

---

(opposite) Musical instruments produce a fundamental frequency together with a series of overtones at lower amplitudes. The number and amplitudes of the overtones determine the quality of the sound and are specific to the particular instrument, thus middle C on a violin will sound different in tone (but not in pitch) from the same note when played on a piano.

the trees. Similarly, a falling object might make a "thud" sound because the impact vibrates the surrounding air. These are situations in which forces of nature cause uncontrolled vibrations that produce *ambient* sound, also known as background noise.

The most complex nature of the sound process is seen in the use of language among humans. Human beings have developed the ability to control sound in a very careful manner, and this has led to the development of numerous languages. Researchers who study speech have pointed out that the English language is made up of about 40 different kinds of *phonemes*, which represent the different

SOUND WAVES

Physicists have shown that sound is a form of wave that travels through a medium, causing the medium to vibrate. As in the case of any other waves, sound waves can be represented by amplitude and frequency. Amplitude refers to the strength of the wave—the taller the wave, the higher its amplitude. The strength of sound waves is measured by a unit called the *decibel* in honor of the physicist Alexander Graham Bell, who was a pioneer in examining the physics of sound. If a sound's decibel level is extremely high, the waves could be so strong that objects being vibrated can be damaged by the sound waves. An eardrum can rupture if a loud noise is produced too close to it. The American Occupational Safety and Health Administration (OSHA) puts a limit on the loudness of a sound to which a factory worker can be exposed. OSHA recommends that workers not be exposed to a continuous sound louder than 90 decibels (the equivalent of a police whistle, heavy traffic, average volume of earphones, some motorcycles at 25 feet (7.6 meters), shouted conversation).

The next characteristic of the sound wave is its frequency, or how fast its vibration moves. Frequency is measured as a number of vibrations per second. This unit of measurement is called a kinds of sounds that a person has to produce to create English words. Phonemes are the smallest units of speech that serve to distinguish one utterance from another in a language or dialect; for instance, the *m* in the word *mat* and the *b* in *bat*.

Other languages might have fewer or more phonemes, as suggested by linguists Morton W. Bloomfield and Leonard Newmark in their 1963 book, *A Linguistic Introduction to the History of English*. According to Bloomfield and Newmark, "The number of phonemes in historical languages seems to range somewhere between 15 and 90." Humans get accustomed to producing the sounds related to

hertz. The scale honors the German physicist Heinrich Rudolf Hertz, who did pioneering work in examining the nature of waves in the late 1800s. Waves of the same frequency sound the same to the human ear. The note "middle C" played on any musical instrument sounds the same because it has a frequency of 262 hertz, which means the eardrum vibrates 262 times per second. The middle C is the first note that piano students are taught to play. In the case of a normal human ear, the frequency range that a person can interpret as sound ranges from 20 hertz to 20,000 hertz. Other animals might be able to hear larger or smaller frequency ranges. For example, a dog is able to hear sounds of up to 100,000 hertz, making it possible to make whistles that produce sound at a frequency only dogs can hear.

The speed of a wave also depends on the medium through which it travels. The standard speed of sound is measured at the altitude of sea level, where sound travels at a speed of about 1,135 feet per second (340 meters per second) in air. This speed varies with temperature, humidity, and the density of air. At higher altitudes, where the air is less dense, the speed of sound is slower. Sound does not travel at all in space since there is no air there. Even though science fiction movies show a lot of sound in space, it is dead silent in reality.

specific languages. Other animals, such as dolphins, can also create sounds that appear to have patterns similar to human languages.

Sound is also produced with tools such as musical instruments, which create specific vibrations in air. A drum produces sound when a person vibrates the stretched leather with his or her hands or a drumstick. Instruments such as the acoustic guitar produce various sounds according to specific string movement. An electric guitar uses an amplifier to produce the sound that is heard since the sound of the string is barely audible by itself. The amplifier on the electric guitar creates the sound by electronically converting the guitar's string vibrations and making them powerful enough to be heard through a loudspeaker. Sounds produced by instruments are usually controlled by a person who has the skills to use an instrument to create vibrations that would sound pleasing to the human ear. The vibrations are eventually picked up by the human ear and one can hear the sound being produced by the instrument.

HOW SOUND IS HEARD

In order for sound to be heard there must be a tool that can sense the waves and be free to vibrate in very precise ways. The sensor also needs to be strong so that constant vibrations do not weaken it, making it unable to sense the range of vibrations that fall on the sensor. The human eardrum is such a sensor that moves with the vibrations around it. Eventually it sends information about the vibrations to the brain through the nerves in the form of electrical energy.

Certain machines can "hear" sound with a sensor that converts sound vibrations into electrical energy. For instance, the telephone has a microphone that is made up of a small vibrating object called a diaphragm, which produces electrical signals. These electrical signals are sent over the telephone wires to another phone. The other phone has a tiny speaker that is made to vibrate in a specific way so that the electrical signals are converted back to sound waves. This process is possible because the amplitude and frequency of a sound wave traveling through air can be converted to electrical energy,

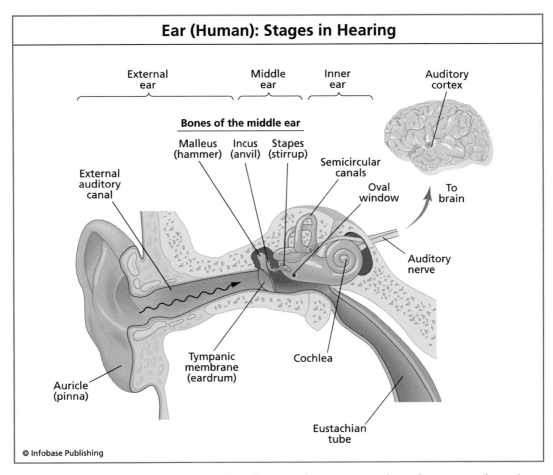

Ear (Human): Stages in Hearing

External ear | Middle ear | Inner ear | Auditory cortex

Bones of the middle ear

Malleus (hammer) | Incus (anvil) | Stapes (stirrup)

Semicircular canals

External auditory canal

Oval window

To brain

Auditory nerve

Tympanic membrane (eardrum)

Cochlea

Auricle (pinna)

Eustachian tube

© Infobase Publishing

In order to hear, the ear detects vibrations and transports them into nerve impulses that are interpreted by the brain as sound. Although a normal ear can identify up to 400,000 sounds, not all sounds can be heard by humans. Dogs are able to hear ultrasound, and snakes sense infrasound through their bellies.

which keeps the characteristics of the sound waves and can travel through wires.

SOUND: AN ANALOGIC PHENOMENON

The German physicist Karl Ferdinand Braun, the winner of the Nobel Prize in Physics in 1909, invented the oscilloscope. This device is used to show the amplitude and frequency of sound waves

THE HUMAN EAR

The first important part of the ear is the ear canal. Sound waves travel through the ear canal and make the eardrum vibrate. These vibrations are sent to the inner ear, which is made up of a delicate combination of three bones. The movement of the eardrum makes these bones vibrate the fluid in the inner ear, which excites specific nerves that carry the information about the vibration to the brain as electrical signals. The brain then interprets the electrical signals as the sound that the person hears. It is this delicate balance of the muscular eardrum, bones, fluids, and nerve cells that allows humans to hear sound.

Although most people can hear sounds, different people have different levels of hearing. For instance, there are some people who are called "tone deaf" because they are unable to distinguish between specific frequencies. This phenomenon can be very severe in some people whose inability to distinguish between frequencies makes it annoying for them to listen to music. A near complete loss of hearing can also be the cause of immense frustration and disadvantages in life. There are many different tools that help people to improve their hearing, such as hearing aids. According to Karl Strom of *The Hearing Review*, "Net hearing instrument unit sales increased by 3.5% to 1.22 million units during the first half of 2007 compared to sales of 1.18 million units in the first half of 2006."

on a screen. The oscilloscope shows that sound waves have a certain height, a certain width, and are also spaced away from each other while they travel at a particular speed. The oscilloscope also shows that louder sounds produce waves with higher peaks, whereas shrill sounds produce waves that are close to each other. The oscilloscope not only helped people to visualize sound, but it also demonstrated that it was possible to assign numbers to measure the size of the waves in terms of their continuously changing amplitude and frequency.

This continuous change makes sound an analogic phenomenon. An analog is a mechanism that represents data by measurement of continuously changing physical quantities such as length, width, voltage, or pressure. Sound waves could have very tiny waves of low amplitude that then become very large waves of high amplitude, just as these waves also have many different frequencies, with the number of waves produced every second varying from low to high numbers. Like sound, most things that are experienced with the senses are analogic. For example, temperature (another analogic phenomenon) is felt as very hot, hot, cool, cold, or very cold. Similarly, taste can vary from being very sweet to somewhat sweet to bitter. An analogic phenomenon can also be measured using instruments such as the speedometer in a car or the thermometer in an oven. These instruments represent the different values of speed or temperature using numbers made up of the traditional 10 digits.

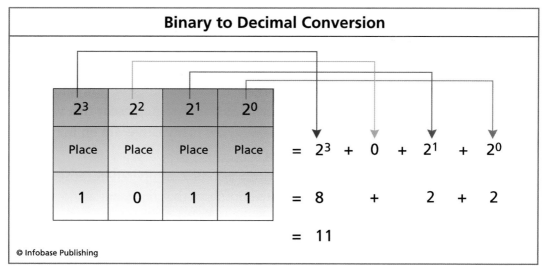

Binary to Decimal Conversion

2^3	2^2	2^1	2^0
Place	Place	Place	Place
1	0	1	1

$= 2^3 + 0 + 2^1 + 2^0$

$= 8 \quad + \quad 2 + 2$

$= 11$

© Infobase Publishing

All digital information is stored as a combination of two digits: 0 and 1. It is possible to convert the information stored as digital information by a simple mathematical process where the digit in the zero place is multiplied with 1. The one in the one place is multiplied by 2, the one in the two place is multiplied by 4 and so on, eventually producing the decimal equivalent of the binary number.

Throughout time, people used the decimal system made up of 10 digits from 0 to 9 to represent changes in a phenomenon. In 1703 German scholar Gottfried Wilhelm Leibniz developed a revolutionary alternative to the decimal number system. He suggested that all numbers could be represented by a system that used two numbers: 0 and 1. This is called a binary system. Leibniz's idea was particularly important since the two digits could be used to describe any situation in terms of a "turned-on" condition represented by the digit 1, or a "turned-off" condition represented by the digit 0. A light switch is a good example of this process, where the switch could be either in the on or off position. A switch that is turned on represents the number 1, whereas a switch that is turned off represents 0. Leibniz's idea did not receive much attention until inventors such as John von Neumann began to think of building counting machines in the early 1900s. The early developers of calculating machines realized that the decimal system was too unwieldy to be used for making calculating machines. They turned to the binary system for simpler manipulation of numbers.

It is very easy to manage binary numbers since one only needs to count how many things are "on" and how many are "off." For instance, it is possible to observe that a room that has five lamps of equal power is very well lit when all the lamps are lit, and not at all well lit when only one lamp is on. If we represent this with the binary system, one would count how many lamps are on in order to say how well the room is lit.

The first step in the process of doing computations with binary numbers is to change decimal numbers that represent analogic situations into their binary equivalents through the process of digitization. This is what happens when the decimal numbers representing the amplitudes and frequencies of sound waves are changed to binary numbers. According to the Institute of Electrical and Electronics Engineers, "Computers rely on binary numbers and binary math because it greatly simplifies their tasks." This simplification is the basis of changing analogic sound into its binary equivalent.

CHANGING DECIMAL NUMBERS TO BINARY

When looking at a two-digit number such as 22, you know that the 2 on the far right is in the ones position and the 2 to the left is in the tens position. School mathematics teaches students to recognize numbers in specific positions such as ones, tens, hundreds, thousands, and so on, so that any number can be broken down into specific parts by looking at the positions of the digits.

The exact same thing happens in the binary system of numbers. In the binary system, the digits are placed in multiples of two, so it goes twos, fours, eights, sixteens, and so on. Since numbers are represented by multiples of two, it is also possible to use only 0 and 1 to represent all numbers. If one wanted to use binary numbers to represent the decimal number 2, it would be written as 10, with a 0 in the ones position and a 1 in the twos position. Using this principle, it is possible to convert any decimal number to a binary equivalent. For example, when converting larger numbers such as the number 22 in the decimal system, more digits are needed to represent the number.

The decimal number 22 becomes 10110 in the binary system. To see how this equals 22, add the binary digits from the left: The first 1 in the sixteens position is added to the 0 in the eights position, and then to the 1 in the fours position, the 1 in the twos position, and finally to the 0 in the ones position, resulting in a total of 22.

This conversion results in the representation of decimal numbers in terms of zeros and ones, which can then become the off and on conditions of an electrical system. For instance, imagine five light bulbs lined up next to one another. The far right bulb represents the ones position, the one to its immediate left is the twos position, and then to its immediate left is the fours position, and so on until the one to the farthest left is the bulb for the sixteens position. Now, by looking at which bulbs are lit, it is possible to determine the decimal number being represented. For example, to represent the decimal number 22 the only bulbs that would be on would be the first, third, and fourth bulbs starting from the far left side.

TURNING ANALOGIC SOUND INTO DIGITAL INFORMATION

To convert analog sound into digital data, one must first measure the characteristics of the sound file in decimal numbers and then convert them to binary numbers. The amplitude of sound waves is measured in decibels with the computer recording a number that represents the decibel level. The frequency of the wave is also recorded as a decimal number. The measurement is done by periodically capturing information about the amplitude and frequency and converting this information to binary numbers.

This process was pioneered by Thomas Stockton in 1963 at the Massachusetts Institute of Technology. Stockton used a machine called an analog to digital converter (ADC) to create digital audio recordings. It took another two decades for digital audio to transform the music industry. In 1981, *BusinessWeek* noted the impact of sound digitization: "In a move that may revolutionize the entire audio industry, Japanese and European manufacturers will soon introduce record players that use the digital language of computers to reproduce the highest-fidelity music yet in this medium. The impact of this move could surpass the stereo transformation that changed the hi-fi business in the 1950s." The process depended largely on the ADC that Professor Stockton used for his pioneering work with the digitization of sound.

The ADC captures the decimal measurements related to a sound wave at rapid intervals, producing an accurate set of numbers that represents the sound wave. The speed at which the measurements are taken is called the sampling rate. It is not unusual to find ADCs that can sample sound 44,000 times per second. At that rate, thousands of decimal numbers are generated, which the ADC converts to their binary equivalents. The machine eventually stores the binary digits as the digitized representation of the analogic sound wave.

The digital version of a sound is not what the original sound was, but is rather a mere sample of the original analog sound. When someone listens to a portable digital music player, these series of numbers are what are being interpreted by the gadget into audible

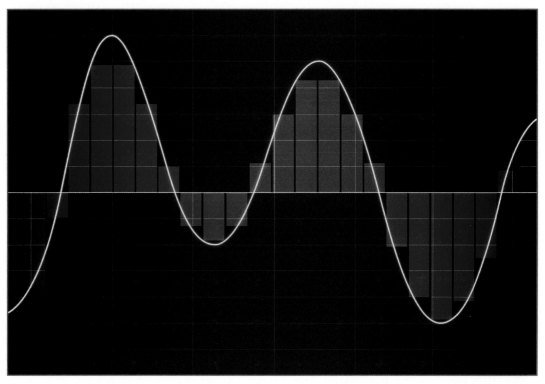

An analog to digital converter converts analog signals into digital numbers. These devices are used to transform sound, movement, and temperature into binary code for the computer. Cell phones, digital cameras, camcorders, and scanners use A/D converters. Above, an A/D converter is transforming sound into binary code.

sound. These numbers can never fully capture the quality of the original sound wave, but the high sampling rate results in minimal loss to the quality of the sound.

This issue of loss of quality has been a key concern with the digitization of sound. Anthony Tommasini, the chief music critic for the *New York Times*, writes:

> Digital recording does indeed sample sound: little slices, called bits, are recorded at the stunning rate of 44,000 times per second. Defenders of the old analog technology used in stereo recordings said that the infinitesimal missing slices of music on CDs undermined the sound quality. Yes, the sound was clear and flawless, but it lacked warmth and richness, they said; it was cold in comparison

COMPRESSING THE SOUND FILE

Because an extremely large set of binary numbers is produced when an ADC digitizes analog music, it is very difficult to manipulate the large numbers. This problem is solved by compressing, or shrinking, the file. The process of compression is a mathematical computation in which the computer does specific calculations to make the digitized music file come down to a manageable size. Later those compressed numbers are passed through a digital to analog converter (DAC), which works as the reverse of the ADC. Then the compressed numbers are interpreted to produce a sound that is very similar to the original music. The process of compression is a significant step in the digitization of sound.

The size of the compressed sound file is also dependent upon how rapidly the sound is sampled: A large sampling rate with little compression produces bigger file sizes that keep the details of the original analog music. On the other hand, highly compressed, smaller files would lead to a noticeable loss in the quality of the sound. For example, a huge compression happens in the case of a digital dictation machine, which a person uses to dictate notes into a tiny gadget. The voice is stored as a sound file. In this case, the sound can be sampled at a lower rate and a massive compression

with the best vinyl recordings played on top-quality stereo systems. That debate has never been settled, though even holdouts for analog technology have to concede that the quality of digital recording has vastly improved over the years.

With ADCs that sample at extremely high rates, the loss is so tiny that the human ear is unable to detect that loss. On the other hand, there are some important gains since digitization produces a digital file that is not much different from any other computer file. Once the computer file has been produced, it is easy to manipulate the file with computer programs such as one called Audacity. Such creates a small file size since quality is unimportant to a dictation machine recording. On the other hand, the sampling is done at a very high rate with minimal compression when classical music is professionally recorded in a music studio.

There are many commonly used compression methods. The Moving Pictures Expert Group (MPEG) offers the mp3 format of sound digitization, which was originally developed in 1987 by the German scientist Dieter Seitzer. The term *mp3* is an abbreviation for MPEG-1 Audio Layer 3, which refers to the type of compression used in creating the mp3 file. The audio layer 3 type of compression keeps most of the sound quality while producing a small enough file size that it can be stored on gadgets such as the iPod.

The importance of compression cannot be underestimated in view of the popularity of portable digital audio players such as the iPod. As pointed out by Kyle Schurman in *Smart Computing* magazine, "Because these portable devices typically have limited storage space, they'll greatly benefit from the increased compression available with mp3 Pro." (The mp3 Pro is an audio compressor that combines the mp3 audio format with a technology that enhances audio, called spectral band replication.) There are several other commonly used methods similar to mp3 that are discussed later in this volume, and they all have the common characteristics of sampling and compression.

programs allow users to cut out segments of sound, add effects such as an echo, or move around sound segments to create new sounds altogether. The computer programs that are used to manipulate sound simply make changes to the numbers in the digital files. Eventually the digital file can also be copied onto gadgets such as iPods. The files can also be sent as e-mail and recorded onto CDs.

The most important aspect of digitization is the fact that the process opens up the possibility of manipulating sound in ways that were not possible with analog sound. The digital information can be altered with easy-to-use computer programs and the files can be shrunk in size for easy storage and sharing.

Making Digital Sound

Digital sound is the product of digitizing analogic sound waves into binary data using a computer system that is able to capture the sound waves and change them into digital information. Scientists in the 1970s pioneered the process of creating digital sound. Digitizing sound has become quite commonplace, and anyone with a computer can create digital sound files. This change has been made possible by several critical developments in computer technology that will be discussed in this chapter.

The process of making digital audio begins with capturing the vibrations that are produced in air when sound is produced. The capturing process correctly records the frequencies and amplitudes of the original vibrations, with little loss in quality. This is done by first converting the vibrations into electrical energy. The strength of the electrical energy is then recorded as binary data. The characteristics of the vibrations finally become numbers made up of 0 and 1.

The most popular tool for capturing sound vibrations is the microphone, which is used to convert vibrations in the surrounding air into electrical signals. The first patented microphone was developed in 1876 by Emile Berliner, who sold the patent to the Bell Telephone Company. Since then, people have constantly improved upon the design. Today there are sophisticated microphones that can capture very tiny vibrations in the air. All microphones have a mechanical part that responds to the vibrations in the surrounding air. In the early days of microphones,

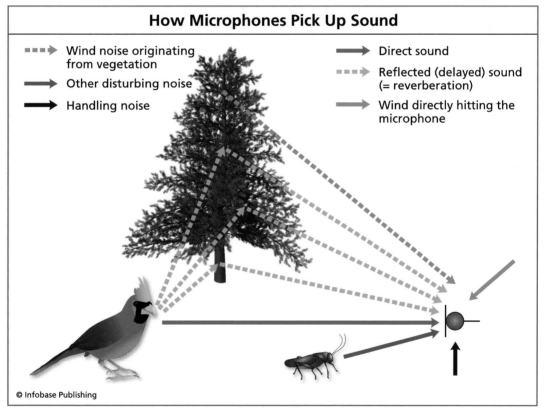

How Microphones Pick Up Sound

- ▶ Wind noise originating from vegetation
- → Other disturbing noise
- → Handling noise

- → Direct sound
- ▶ Reflected (delayed) sound (= reverberation)
- → Wind directly hitting the microphone

© Infobase Publishing

The sound picked up by a microphone that is operated outside is made up of many different components. Usually the goal is to pick up the direct sound from the source that is the center of attention, but other sounds called "ambient noise" are also picked up. Sometimes the ambient noise makes the primary sound appear more realistic.

this mechanical part was a sheet of metal called a diaphragm, which would move with the movements in the surrounding air. The metal sheet was later replaced by metal ribbons, tiny crystals, and other objects that had the ability to move in sync with the vibrations in the air. These vibrations would produce an electrical current whose magnitude would depend on the strength of vibrations picked up by the microphone. The amount of electrical energy coming out of the microphone would indicate the amplitude and frequency of the sound that caused the vibrations of the diaphragm. The information about the electrical signal is sent to a computer that converts the electrical analog information into binary digital information. The quality of the digital information is dependent upon how well the microphone is able to convert the sound waves into electrical energy.

This conversion process has seen several developments. For example, the sensitivity of microphones has increased. The early microphones had diaphragms that could only vibrate within certain frequency ranges, missing sounds in the higher and lower tonal levels. These kinds of microphones were used in telephones but were useless for capturing music. New microphones had to be developed when radio became popular and radio stations were interested in broadcasting live music programs. Even though radio did not digitize the sound, there was a need for high-quality microphones to efficiently capture it.

With the developments in the engineering of microphones, it was possible to make more sensitive diaphragms. This allowed for a larger range of sounds to be captured, with the invention of the microphone leading to the development of specialized microphones for different kinds of tasks. For example, it is possible to use a computer as a voice recognition tool: The computer is able to understand commands sent to it by a person speaking into a microphone. In this case the computer would interpret the binary file produced by the voice as a specific command. These specific needs have led to a particular specialization in microphone design with a specific emphasis on making the microphones smaller without losing quality.

TYPES OF MICROPHONES

The microphone is a device that is used to convert sound waves into electrical energy. All types of microphones must have a part that is able to vibrate when sound waves in the surrounding air strike it. There must also be another part of the microphone that converts the vibrations into electrical signals.

Microphones are classified in several ways: First, different types of microphones can pick up sounds from different directions. Sound waves are created all the time as objects make the surrounding air vibrate, with the vibrations coming from different directions. The human ear has evolved to a point where it can pick up vibrations from different directions, and people can tell from which direction a sound is coming. Some types of microphones are also designed to pick up sound waves from different directions. For example, the omni-directional microphone will pick up sound from any direction, whereas the unidirectional microphone will pick up sound from only one direction. Each type of microphone has its specific uses. The unidirectional

A microphone converts sound into an electrical signal. Microphones were first used with early telephones. Today, there are all types—dynamic, condenser, and ribbon microphones—that are used for specific jobs.

microphone is used in conditions where the amount of ambient sound captured by the microphone must be low so that the microphone can capture the sound from a specific source. This is especially important with the microphone of a cell phone, which should not pick up all the sounds surrounding the user of the phone, but only what the caller is saying.

Second, microphones vary in size. The older ones, which were based on a vibrating diaphragm

(continues)

(continued)

and carbon dust, are usually larger. New technologies have made microphones and their vibrating elements smaller, which is demanded by the miniaturization of many gadgets. These microphones might not even use large diaphragms. Condenser microphones use tiny, thin, vibrating metal sheets. Crystal microphones use a special kind of crystalline mineral that is sensitive to vibrations in the air. Miniaturization has not led to a loss of quality. Some of the smaller microphones are just as sensitive as the larger ones. The process of miniaturization has allowed the microphone to be embedded in many different gadgets.

It is expected that microphones will become smaller, more sensitive, and more affordable, so that the option to capture sound can be built into many different tools. Whenever there is a need to capture any kind of sound, there is a need for a microphone.

The increasing popularity of portable digital devices such as cell phones led to the need for good microphones that could fit in small gadgets. These kinds of microphones also convert vibrations into electrical energy, but they do so without the use of the traditional diaphragm. In the smaller microphones the vibrations are captured by other tools, such as an electrical device called a condenser. A condenser is able to accurately convert sound wave vibrations into electrical energy. All microphones serve the basic function of converting sound energy into electrical energy. The microphone is essential for capturing sound that exists as vibrations in the air. The captured sound can then be digitized to produce a digital file.

It is also possible to capture digital sound without a microphone: The digital information is created by a computer using specific programs that generate the digital files. The digital files represent different kinds of sound. This will be discussed in the next section.

CREATING NEW SOUNDS

Digital sound is made up of a set of numbers that digital to analog converters (DACs) use to reproduce the original sounds. Since the DAC only works with numbers, it is possible to input a set of numbers that the DAC would make into sound, creating sounds that have no familiarity with natural sounds. Such sounds begin as numbers generated by computer programs.

The ability to digitally produce new sounds opens up a creative possibility where the musician can produce music with only a computer and different digital files that can be combined to produce sounds that appear to be from different sources. Using this method the digital musician can produce any sound, from that of a traditional guitar to that of drums, and then combine them together to produce the sound of a band. For example, a Web-based program called Fractal Music Generator allows people to use a simple set of instructions to compose music by selecting pre-programmed music segments. Using such programs, anyone can produce a complete musical piece without ever touching a real instrument.

The ability to create sounds using digital information has been a great asset for the visually impaired. For example, this technology can be used to help people who are unable to read a computer screen. Special screen-reader software enables them to listen, rather than see, what is on the screen. This software is also used by businesspeople for easy access to their information. A company called jConnect offers Jtalk, a service that uses text-to-speech technology to read your e-mail messages to you over the phone. Such services have become increasingly popular as the technology to produce digital sound has become sophisticated and affordable.

SAMPLING AND COMBINING

Digital systems deal with sound in the form of a specific number sequence, which can be combined to create new sound. It is now possible to combine parts of different sound sequences to make a

THE SYNTHESIZER

The synthesizer creates sound by manipulating electrical energy with an electronic device called an oscillator. The person using the synthesizer is able to control the electrical energy by using keys, like those used on a piano, which are connected to the oscillator circuits inside the synthesizer.

The first analog synthesizer, built in 1876 by Elisha Grey, was a device similar to a telephone and was capable of producing sounds in specific frequencies. Although there were small developments in synthesizer technology in the century following its invention, the real boost came when Robert Moog developed the electric circuits that produced sounds that could be used by musicians. The Moog synthesizer was soon adopted by rock musicians such as the Monkees in 1967. Since then the synthesizer has become standard equipment for many musicians.

There are two kinds of synthesizers that musicians can use. First is the traditional synthesizer, which was based on analog technology where the user directly manipulates the electrical voltage flowing through the oscillator. The varying voltage passed through the oscillator to produce electrical energy. The electrical energy then made the speaker move in such a way that the sound frequency associated with the electrical energy was heard. The synthesizer operated as an analog device in which the speakers converted the continuously varying electrical energy into sound.

completely new sound file. The process of using sequences from different sources is called sampling. (This should not be confused with the sampling that refers to the way sound is digitized.) Sampling involves selecting bits of music from different sources and combining them in the production of new music. The process consists of two steps. First, some recorded sound (such as an old song,

The modern synthesizer uses digital technology with computer programs built into the synthesizer to produce specific electrical signals. Since the digital synthesizer is based on computer programs, it is possible to build one into an existing computer. For example, the company Propellerhead, based in Sweden, has developed a computer program called Reason. The latest version is a multi-synthesis synthesizer with six oscillator types, four different filters, a step sequencer and a modulation matrix. It is fully routable, fully automatable, fully everything. This complex system is available on CDs and the user has to install the program on a computer to begin using the digital synthesizer and related tools. This technology allows for greater flexibility since the computer can be instructed to produce many different kinds of sounds.

Digital synthesizers that are stand-alone machines also offer a significant amount of creative opportunities. This power has been translated into creative music that would have been simply impossible without the synthesizer.

Synthesizers are electronic instruments that produce a wide range of sounds and imitate other instruments with varying degrees of accuracy. Some musicians use synthesizers in place of actual instruments, such as the saxophone, harmonica, flute, or guitar.

a specific drum roll, or a natural sound) is re-recorded, keeping a small portion of the original sound in the re-recording. The second step involves either repeating the same piece of recorded music or combining many different segments in order to produce a longer piece of music. Eventually the new music does not resemble the original at all.

Sampling and re-combining was used before digital music was available. In the 1950s songwriter Dickie Goodman started the trend of taking snippets from existing songs and combining them to produce completely new songs. The process was then adapted by DJs such as Kool Herc from Jamaica, who used this system in the 1970s by concurrently playing multiple turntables in New York City dance clubs.

Although the DJs of the 1970s did not have computers, they sampled and created new music by playing pieces of existing music in different sequences while adding new lyrics to the music. Today, digital technology has made the process of sampling much simpler. With a computer, sampling can be done more precisely since the musician now is able to select very tiny segments of music. The tiny bits of sampled music are then available for many kinds of manipulation. The musician is able to change the frequency and amplitude of the sampled sound to create a new kind of sound. Artists' creativity and the opportunities offered by digital technology contributed to the development of hip-hop music. In his book *Making Beats: The Art of Sample-based Hip-hop*, hip-hop scholar Joseph Glenn Schloss describes the use of technology by hip-hop artists and suggests that creating this music requires significant creative talent as well as access to powerful computers that can do all the different required tasks.

COMPUTERS FOR DIGITAL SOUND

In 2004, Jesse Nieminen of *Digital Web Magazine* stated that digital audio work required a computer that could be dedicated to only dealing with digitized sound files. This recommendation is based on the fact that the computer for digital audio must have capabilities that are not available on a regular computer. First, the computer for digital audio must have a good sound card. A sound card is a circuit board that can be inserted into the computer motherboard, or main board of the computer, to create and record real, high-quality sound.

The sound card acts as the ADC for the computer by taking analog electrical signals from a device such as a microphone and sending them directly into the computer. The sound card has sockets where the cables from other analog sound devices such as a microphone, tape recorder, or audio amplifier can be connected to the computer. Better sound cards can rapidly sample the incoming analog signal to convert it into digital information. Higher sampling rates result in better sound quality, and good sound cards are also able to handle a large range of sound frequencies.

The computer must also have the appropriate software to record the digital information that is being captured by the sound card. There are many different programs that do this with varying degrees of sophistication. Some of the programs allow for the recording of only a very short segment of sound, whereas others can record long segments. For example, computers using Microsoft Windows have a simple sound recorder built into the system that can only record a sound segment of up to one minute long. Programs such as Audacity, however, allow for capturing full songs. Audacity also allows the user to edit the sound file that is captured. The user can clean out background noise that had been created in the file or add special effects to the sound by overlaying modifications such as an echo effect on top of the recorded sound.

The computer must also have enough memory so that the digital sound file can be stored, since the high-quality sound files can become very large. The computer needs to be able to store and quickly retrieve this large amount of information. The files are usually stored on the hard drive of the computer, where the information must be recorded in real time. Sometimes the hard drive of the computer is not fast enough to keep up with the speed at which the information is being captured. In such cases, a buffer must be set up where temporary information is stored before it is recorded on the hard drive.

All of these requirements result in a complicated computer, and the typical personal computer is usually not fully equipped to do

(continues on page 38)

SPEAKERS

The speaker converts electrical signals into vibrations that can be heard by the human ear. Speakers come in many different sizes, ranging from massive units used in public performances or concerts to tiny headphones that are used with portable music players, to medium-sized speakers used with home music systems. All speakers do the same task: They use the electrical signal to make an object vibrate, essentially reversing the operation of the microphone. Speakers can be categorized based on the specific way in which they would be used. The use could be dependent upon the number of people who would need to hear the sound coming from the speaker.

Headphones are smaller speakers that are used to create private listening spaces. The development of headphone technology is progressing every year. Some modern headphones actively cancel out external sounds, creating a sound bubble where the listener is completely cut off from his or her surrounding sound environment.

The alternative to this is to have speakers that produce a sound that can be heard in the space surrounding the speaker. This technology is used when the sound is shared with others, so several people in one space can all listen to the same music. The speakers used for this purpose are larger than headphone speakers and can create an environment where the listeners would feel surrounded by sound of a very high quality.

Finally, there are conditions in which large speakers are used for open spaces where many people need to be able to hear the sound. This is the case in a movie theater, a public concert, or public meeting. These events need larger speakers mounted strategically so that the sound is heard clearly all throughout the large space. In all of these cases, the speaker is the final connection between audio devices and the human ear, which makes it really important that the speaker be able to accurately reproduce the sound waves that are represented by the electrical signals.

Amar Bose of the Massachusetts Institute of Technology invented a speaker system that has gone on to become one of the best lines of speakers in the world. In 1999, MIT

Parts of a Speaker

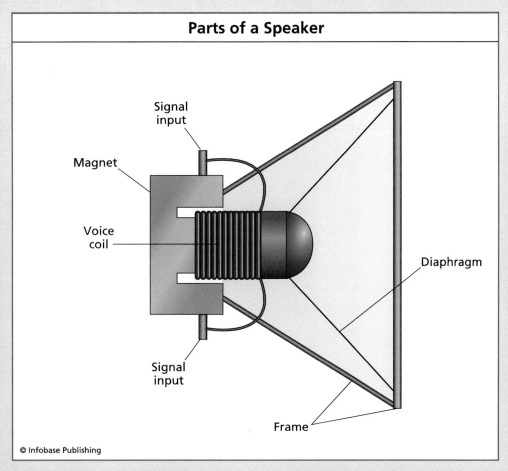

Signal input

Magnet

Voice coil

Diaphragm

Signal input

Frame

© Infobase Publishing

The speaker is the most important tool for converting electrical information into audible sound. This is done with the combination of a flexible diaphragm that vibrates when the voice coil of the speaker is made to move by the electrical signals that reach the voice coil. The vibrations of the diaphragm make the air vibrate, producing the sound.

noted that, "Amar Bose has earned over two dozen patents, and he still works full time, directing a more than $550 million company, whose products can be found in Olympics stadiums, Broadway theatres, the Sistine Chapel, and the Space Shuttle (where his noise cancellation system protects the astronauts from permanent hearing damage)."

(continued from page 35)
all the tasks. When dealing with professional digital audio it is important to have not only the necessary audio equipment, but also a computer that can deal with the complex sound file that is created by the process of digitization. These special, complex files will be discussed in the next chapter.

What Is a
Digital Sound File?

In a 2006 *Washington Post* article, technology commentator Mike Musgrove spoke of the various formats in which digital music is available to the consumer. He wrote, "Thanks to competing file formats and business models, the digital music world can be a little confusing—and it's about to get more so."

As pointed out in Chapter 2, the digitization process samples from analog sound waves and stores some of the information while leaving out other pieces. The result is that the digitized sound is somewhat inferior in quality to the original sound. The quality of the sound suffers further when the large digital file created from the sampling process has to be stored on the computer, because the size of the file produced by digitization is usually very large. For example, a single minute of digitized sound could take up the same space on a computer hard drive as 50 books, like this one, do on a shelf. The storage of sound files requires that the file size be made smaller, resulting in a loss of quality through a

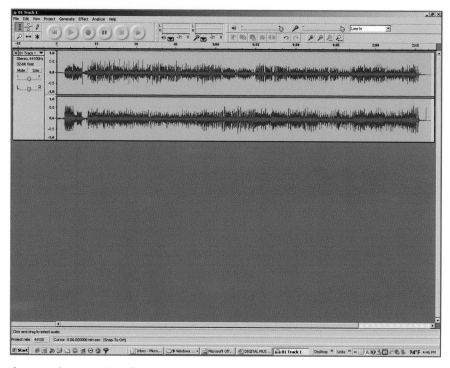

A sound, or audio, file stores audio data on a computer. The data is compressed to reduce the file size. There are several types of audio file formats, including the Wave, which was developed by Microsoft. A Wave file (identified by its file extension .wav) has become the standard PC audio file format for everything from video games to CDs.

process of compression. Mathematical computations are used to make the digitized file smaller.

PC Magazine Encyclopedia describes audio compression as a process that formats audio data to take up less storage space. Compression typically removes some of the audio data, assuming that an average person is unable to notice small losses in the quality of music. Although there is some loss in quality, the process of compression makes it possible to use digital audio in everyday life because uncompressed digital files would be unmanageably large.

The debate over the acceptable amount of quality loss has resulted in different kinds of compression. Some methods compress and store the file with virtually no loss in quality, whereas other formats lead to significant losses in quality that a listener would clearly notice. These two kinds of compression—called "lossless" and "lossy"—are described by Bruce Fries, the author of the book *Digital Audio Essentials.* He explains:

> Lossless formats store digital audio with absolutely no loss of information. Some, like PCM, store just the raw audio data with no compression, while others like Apple Lossless and FLAC use lossless compression techniques to create files about half the size of files that use plain PCM. Lossy formats like MP3, AAC, Ogg Vorbis, and WMA can achieve much larger reductions in file size than are possible with lossless compression. By discarding unnecessary and redundant information, lossy formats can squeeze an audio file to less than one tenth of its original size without losing much quality.

The key to the process of compression is achieving a balance between quality of sound and the size of the file, since larger files could be difficult to manage.

SIZE OF DIGITAL SOUND FILES

To understand why digital sound files can become very large it is important to remember that all digital information is stored in binary form as a 0 or 1. The numbers of 0s and 1s in a file are reported as either the bit or the byte. The smallest unit of storage is called a bit, which represents one of the two binary numbers. The string of numbers that is produced by combining eight bits placed next to one another is called a byte. The term *byte* was first used in 1956 by scientists at IBM and is now the standard way of referring to digital file sizes.

Since all digital files are fundamentally made of binary digits, the combination of the terms *bit* and *byte* helps to create a standard reference to the size of a file. Byte is the preferred way to refer to file size because digital information is typically stored in combinations of eight bits. For example, if it were necessary to store the number 6 in binary format, it would be converted to its binary equivalent (110). In the eight-bit system these digits would make up a single byte of data in which the eight bits would appear as 00000110. Each of the 0s and 1s represent a bit of information, while the eight bits together represent a byte of information. In this fashion, many numbers can be stored using the eight-bit byte.

When analog music is digitized, millions of analog numbers representing specific amplitudes and frequencies are converted into binary information, producing an extremely large number of bytes. A three-minute song could easily become a file requiring 4,450,000 bytes, or close to 4.5 megabytes (also called MB). This means that nearly 45 MB of files would be produced if 10 three-minute songs were digitized. Computers available in the early 2000s were typically sold with hard drives that could store about 20,000 MB of information. If the entire hard drive were used for storing digitized audio files, then 4,000 to 5,000 compressed digital songs could be stored on the hard drive. At the same time, filling up the hard drive of a computer with music will make the computer useless for all other work, since the same hard drive is required for other computer activities as well.

Just like a bookshelf can hold only a limited number of books, a hard drive can hold only a limited number of files. The demand for storage space is somewhat eased by the fact that technological improvements are making hard drives more affordable. Affordable hard drives allow users to store more bytes on the drive. The best way to maximize the number of files stored is to find different ways of storing information without any noticeable loss in the quality of the information. According to Brad Miser and Tim Robertson in their book *iPod and iTunes Starter Kit,* "When it comes to digital audio files, one trade-off always has to be made. And that is file size versus sound quality." The hard drive is a limited resource that must also hold all the programs required to operate the computer as well as digital audio files.

RECORDING DIGITAL SOUND IN DIFFERENT FORMATS

The process of digitization produces binary data that is compressed for storage. The compressed file is later used to extract audio information so that sound waves can be created. The cycle of digitization begins with encoding the sound wave information into the digital format and later decoding the digital information to recreate the sound waves using an instrument, such as a speaker. The way in which encoding and decoding is done is called the codec. Most computers are able to digitize music using different codecs and the format of the resulting sound file depends on the specific codec that is used. There are many different codecs that can be used for creating audio files. The choice of the codec results in a specific music file format, so it is important to have some criteria in mind when selecting the codec.

One of the most important factors to consider in choosing the codec is how many ways the resulting format might be used. For example, if the final digital product is not compatible for use on many computers, the user will have to use only a specific kind of computer to replay the digital audio file. Some codecs produce formats that are more universal than others, making it possible to share sounds easily between computers. For example, most computers would be able to decode music that has been encoded into the mp3 format.

Another important factor that helps to determine the choice of codec and the resulting format is the desired quality of the recording. There are codecs that use very little compression, meaning that all the small details of the sampled music are kept. Other codecs produce lower quality recordings that would barely retain the quality of the original analog sound. The choice between the different qualities is related to the issue of size. The codecs that produce better quality result in larger files. The codecs that result in poor sound quality require less computing power and produce smaller files.

One important thing to note about the choice of codec is that a format that creates a smaller file size by removing segments of the audio information through the process of compression can never be

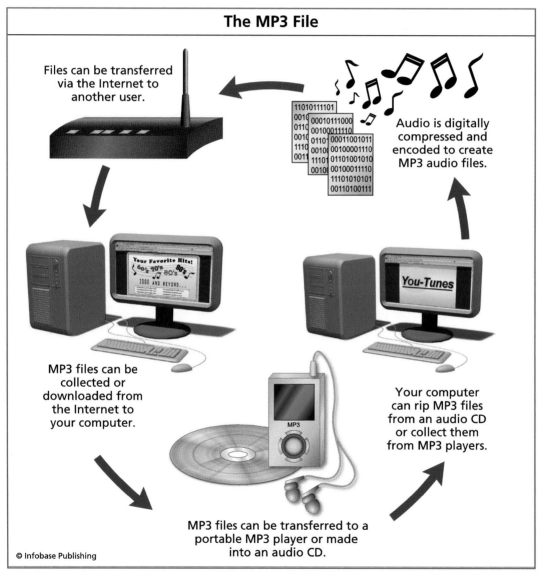

The MP3 File

Files can be transferred via the Internet to another user.

Audio is digitally compressed and encoded to create MP3 audio files.

MP3 files can be collected or downloaded from the Internet to your computer.

Your computer can rip MP3 files from an audio CD or collect them from MP3 players.

MP3 files can be transferred to a portable MP3 player or made into an audio CD.

© Infobase Publishing

The most common type of digital audio file is the mp3 format. It can be produced by most computers, then transferred to other audio devices, such as digital personal music players and digital cameras, and shared with other users.

used to recover the original sound. The loss in quality is permanent. It is not possible to go from lossy back to lossless—those crystalline highs and gut-shaking lows found in a song's details are gone forever. This means that users need to be somewhat careful about the kind of codec and format chosen because it can be very difficult to move from one format to another after the original analog music has been digitized using a specific codec.

The lack of consistency and the existence of multiple formats have led to a competition among the formats. Some of them have become more popular than others. As a result of the competition, consumers are forced to sift through all the options and are sometimes confused about the best choice of codec and format.

FORMAT COMPATIBILITY

Musicians and producers have developed their own ways of encoding, compressing, and decoding digital sound, resulting in the emergence of many different formats. The end result of all the competing processes is a binary file, regardless of the format used. The binary file is constructed in different ways, depending on the method of encoding used. The encoding method also determines the kind of decoding program that would be needed to read the file. Just as a key is specific to a lock, the decoding program is specific to the corresponding encoding program. The issue of compatibility becomes important because decoding programs are only able to read files created in compatible formats.

The reading limitation exists partly because the companies that market the software are often interested in ensuring that their software gains more customers. If a software manufacturer wants its users to only use its codec, then that codec would be built into a computer. When the user wants to digitize music, that codec would automatically start up, producing the digitized file—but it would work well only on machines that use that particular software. This results in major technology corporations battling to maintain the supremacy of their preferred format. As Jay Lyman writes in *TechNewsWorld*, "Apple is credited with gaining the dominant position in the online music category with its successful iPod player and iTunes Music Store—which led the way with the 99-cent song model—but Microsoft has managed to make its WMA format the standard of most other online music services and digital players." This ongoing rivalry is an inconvenience to users who must familiarize themselves with the different formats and buy the computer programs that can decode files in different formats.

Part of this tension is resolved by universal codecs that are developed by scientists who are not connected to any particular technology corporation. The most popular format is endorsed by the Motion Picture Experts Group (MPEG), who offered the MP3 codec and format for digitizing sound. Files of this format can be decoded by most music programs.

The lack of compatibility among the different formats has also led to the development of many software products that can convert digitized files from one format to another. For example, the format used in the CD has been globally standardized, leading to the development of computer programs that convert the CD format to the mp3 format by compressing the digital audio information on the CD into the smaller mp3 format. There are other, similar computer programs that convert files from one format to another, although it is still impossible to move from a lossy format to a lossless format.

It is unclear if any single format will eventually become standardized, because all the formats have advantages and disadvantages. Some are suitable for music while others do better with other kinds of sounds. Eventually the formats would most likely be selected based on the purpose of digitization. The need for good quality would require a specific format, whereas other formats would produce smaller, more manageable files when quality is unimportant.

EMERGENCE OF STANDARDIZED FORMATS

The confusion over audio file formats has led to developers trying to establish standard formats for digitizing music. There are three main groups involved in the standardization efforts: those who look at the issue of format purely as a matter of finding the best encoding/decoding technology; those who are interested in marketing their own format; and professional organizations that are able to describe specific criteria that need to be met for a format to be accepted.

All of these groups have been at work in the standardization of digital music design, resulting in the emergence of three popular formats. One of these formats has been standardized by the development of the CD. The CD format has become popular because it was the first efficient digital format that made use of a sophisticated technological process. The quality of the music on a CD is very good because of the high sampling rate that is used to create the digital file, even though the quality results in large files. The large file size means that only a limited amount of digitized sound can be stored on a CD and the user needs to have multiple CDs in order to store a large collection of music.

The music industry favors this format and has converted nearly all music to it, using CDs as the main way of distributing music. The CD format replaced vinyl albums and cassettes, and consumers rapidly adopted the CD. There was also a boom in the development of numerous CD players, which ranged from very sophisticated CD players meant for professional use to small portable machines that were developed so that people could easily carry the player with them. In the more than 20 years since the first CD was sold, nearly 12 billion CDs have been sold.

The main disadvantage of the CD was that it was not possible to store more than a limited amount of music on one disc. The drawback was addressed by the development of a specific codec for sound. MPEG, which is a part of the International Standards Organization, an international body that sets standards for technologies, supported a codec that was able to take the digital file on a CD or sound from other sources and reduce the file size significantly without too much noticeable drop in the quality of the sound. The resulting small file was named the mp3 file. The mp3 file was also small enough to be used in many different ways.

For example, the mp3 file could be sent over the Internet, stored on computer hard drives without using up too much memory, or stored on portable music players. Other software developers quickly produced small, simple programs that could decode the smaller mp3 file to reproduce the sound.

Although the MPEG group supported the mp3 format, other industry groups (particularly companies that were already in the business of developing software) began to release their own formats. Among these was iTunes Advanced Audio Coding (AAC), which was developed with the cooperation of German engineering society Fraunhofer IIS, AT&T Bell Laboratories, and audio specialists Dolby Laboratories, Sony Corporation, and Nokia. MPEG officially declared it an international standard in 1997.

AAC is a standardized lossy compression and encoding system for digital audio. It achieves better sound quality at similar bit rates as the mp3. At the beginning of its development, there was a disadvantage because the AAC format could be played only on iPods but not on other digital music players. Apple then allowed some other gadgets, such as the Sony PlayStation 3, to play the AAC format. There are competing forces at work to see what becomes standardized. Until that standardization happens, it would be necessary to have access to multiple digital hardware/software combinations to play music digitized in different ways.

One ongoing challenge is finding adequate computer memory to store all the files that are being produced as more and more music is digitized. This need makes computer memory one of the most important hardware pieces necessary to enjoy digital music.

COMPUTER MEMORY TO STORE SOUND

There are several critical concerns about storing digital sound files, starting with the issue of portability. The CD is portable media since it is easy to carry a CD player with oneself. The portable CD player followed the trend of the portable cassette player, which was popularized by products such as the Sony Walkman. The companies that made portable cassette players also started making portable CD

COMPACT DISC

In March 1982, the compact disc was introduced in the United States, and shortly thereafter in Asia. Since then, the CD has become the standardized media for recording digital audio.

(continues)

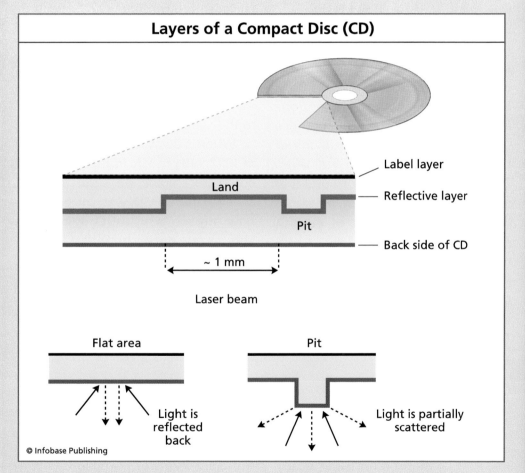

Layers of a Compact Disc (CD)

Label layer

Land

Reflective layer

Pit

Back side of CD

~ 1 mm

Laser beam

Flat area

Light is reflected back

Pit

Light is partially scattered

© Infobase Publishing

A CD is made from plastic, with a thin layer of aluminum applied to the surface to make it reflective. The label serves as a protector that covers the pits, which are encoded with data. A laser beam reads the CD, and a sensor converts this information into electronic data.

(continued)

A compact disc is made of a plastic circle 4.7 inches (120 millimeters) in diameter that is coated with several different layers of material, starting with the label layer where the name of the CD is printed. On the other side of the plastic is a layer made of a metal such as aluminum or gold, upon which the sound data is embedded as a series of tiny indentations. In the language of CD engineers, these indentions are often called pits. Since these pits are extremely tiny, millions of them can be put on the metal layer. The entire CD is filled with pits that are arranged in a spiral of tracks that begin at the center of the CD. All the pits are covered with a protective layer of clear plastic.

When a CD is inserted into a CD player, a laser beam is pointed at the data layer, which reflects the laser. The direction of the reflected laser depends on where the beam falls: If the beam falls on a pit, the reflected light comes back at a different angle than it would if it hit the non-pit surface of the CD. The CD player is able to detect if the laser beam was reflected by a pit or a non-pit surface, interpreting the reflection as either a 0 or 1 digit of binary data. The DAC of the CD player decodes this information and converts the digital information into electrical signals. The electrical signals are sent to the speaker to produce music.

When CDs were first introduced in 1982, only music industry experts could put music on CDs. In 1990 a new kind of CD was introduced; now anyone with a CD writer was able to put music on writable CDs. This process was especially popular because most computers sold in the late 1990s had CD writers installed in them, allowing users to make their own CDs.

players. These products continue to be very popular, with electronic stores advertising nearly 25 different kinds of portable CD players in 2007.

The disadvantage of CD storage, however, is its space limitations. A CD can hold between 70 to 80 minutes of digital music, which amounts to about 20 songs. As the demand rose for carrying around larger amounts of music, it was clear that the memory to store digitized music had to be small in physical size, large enough to hold numerous digital files, and durable enough to withstand shocks related to movement.

The need for miniaturization, capacity, and durability gave rise to the form of memory called flash memory. This technology was pioneered by Japanese scientist Fujio Masuoka in the 1970s, but not even his employer Toshiba Electronics paid much attention to this invention at first. Eventually, in 1988, the technology that stored information on microprocessors was improved upon by the American microprocessor manufacturer Intel Corporation.

Flash memory does not have any moving parts and the digital information is recorded as computer code on the microchip. As long as a sufficient number of microprocessors can be crammed into a small space, it is possible to store any kind of digital information on a flash memory. This method offers great durability but is limited by the amount of files that can be stored on each flash memory based on the size of the music files and the size of the flash memory (usually measured in gigabytes, or one million bytes). Affordable flash memory cards hold about 300 songs and more expensive ones hold up to 1,500 songs. On the other hand, flash memory cards can be used with any computer, so music can be encoded using a lossy compression process. This means that even the less expensive flash memory can accommodate many more music files than what could be stored on a normal commercial CD.

Since 1988, flash memory has played a significant role in a variety of digital applications. "Think of the things that have become common in the United States that either did not exist, or were very rare before 1980 due to cost, practicality, and technological barriers: the personal computer, PDAs, laptops, mobile phones, digital cameras, USB flash drives, and iPods," wrote Lynn Erla Beegle on *TMCnet*. "Each of these devices owes their useful existence to the invention of the non-volatile flash memory." Even though flash memory provides a durable and portable memory device for storing digital audio files, it still does not fully address the issue of capacity.

The demand for larger memory space is met by another kind of device: the mini hard drive. It is similar to the hard drive that is

Flash memory cards store and transfer data between computers and other digital devices. These cards are popular because they are easy to use, do not require power to maintain the information on the card, and can withstand extremes in temperature, immersion in water, and intense pressure.

inside a computer. A mini hard drive requires a moving part, since a hard drive must rotate. These small drives are often placed in shock-proof casings to be able to withstand environmental impact.

The development of the mini hard drive changed the way in which digital music was consumed because these drives made it possible to carry around very large amounts of music. People could now have access to hundreds of CDs in a tiny hard drive. A culture of personalized music consumption developed around this storage system, where every person was able to listen to a customized sound. This memory solution addressed almost all the issues related to storing digital music files. For example, many portable music players are built around these hard drives, with the capacity of the hard drives constantly growing, as pointed out by technology reviewer Donald Bell of *CNET.com* magazine. "High-capacity hard-drive digital-audio players are the kings of mp3 land," Bell wrote. "From a modest 5GB [gigabyte] a few years back to up to 160GB today, hard-drive-based players still give you the most bang for your buck. You can now carry your entire music or media library in a device that has shrunk over time."

Digital sound can also be stored on the traditional computer hard drive where all other digital information resides. The storage space is often very large, so huge amounts of music can be stored there. These hard drives are part of a computer system, and music-editing computer programs can be used to manipulate a stored music file. This will be discussed in the next section.

MANIPULATING SOUND FILES

One of the most common ways to manipulate a sound file is to simply remove a part of the file and take away a complete segment of the sound. Parts of a digital file can be cut out very easily using simple computer programs that allow for editing sound files. The whole process of cutting out can be done on the computer screen just by looking at a visual representation of the sound. These visual representations can show the sound in great detail, allowing tiny segments of it to be removed. This process is often used when a recorded sound has glitches that came up during the recording. For example, when doing an interview there might be vocal elements such as "umm" that can be cleaned out of the digital audio file without the listener ever noticing the editing.

The second form of cutting removes a particular part of a sound file without removing other parts. It is possible to remove the entire vocal section of a song by picking out the digital representation of the specific vocal frequencies and deleting that part while keeping all the other sounds. An entire set of frequencies can be removed from the stored digital file. Karaoke music is often created this way.

There are computer programs that can be used to remove specific frequencies from a sound file. This is sometimes used in law enforcement activities when specific parts of an audio recording need to be separated from the background noise. Enhancedaudio.net offers audio restoration software, describing it as a "unique and powerful tool capable of recovering speech from recordings containing loud music or other coherent noise. Until now, a recording that was covered or masked by loud music was basically a lost cause. DSS decoding is designed to make it possible to attenuate [turn down] this music and uncover the speech." This is possible only because the sound can be digitized into binary data, which can then be analyzed by tools such as DSS.

A third form of manipulation involves adding information such as sound effects or new instruments to the digital sound file to enhance the original sound. Professional musicians often do this when they record different parts of a song as different digital files. These different parts are eventually mixed together to produce the final sound. A mixture could also include visual information, with specific pictures or videos being added to the digital sound file. It is easy to mix different sets of digital information to create a new file, as long as what is being added is available in a digital format. Mixing is often used in the creation of files such as computer-generated music videos that are made up of sound and images connected together in a seamless way.

The fact that digital sound can be manipulated so easily raises issues about the authenticity of the sound one hears. It is never clear whether the sound that is being played from a digital file is something that was originally recorded from an analog source. The very notion of "original" becomes difficult to define since the final sound could have been intentionally manipulated. Digitization and manipulation of sound can create new kinds of sound that might never be found in the realm of the analog or real life, but may be created using many different kinds of tools and applications.

COMBINING SOUND WITH OTHER INFORMATION

Digitized sound files can be placed on small computer chips that can be embedded into different tools, resulting in gadgets that can talk to the user. There are talking household appliances such as toasters that can understand spoken commands. Voice recognition is done by digitizing the sound of the command, and the digital file is then used to instruct a computer program to control the appliance. For example, when the microphone in the toaster hears the sound "on" it creates the binary data related to the sound. This binary data is interpreted as the instruction to turn on the toaster. These appliances are also able to talk back to the user using digitized sound.

The British Broadcasting Corporation (BBC) reports that there has been interest in developing more of these gadgets: "Talking fridges and intelligent boilers could become standard household appliances as the UK Government announces a £40m (40 million British pounds) spend on new technologies." The potential of combining digital audio with analog tools is extensive since speaking is a more natural way of interaction than using a keyboard and mouse. Digitized sound is the future tool for interacting with machines.

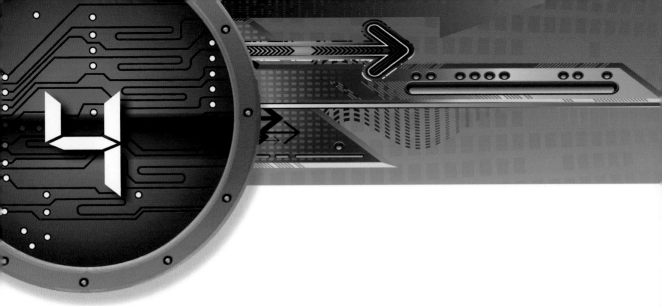

Listening to Digital Sound

I n 2007 *Time* magazine listed the top 10 gadgets of the year and included two digital music players, with the Apple iPhone taking the first position in the list. That same year, a Web-based service called eMusic, which sells digital music on the Internet, reported that it had sold 150 million downloads of music within the first six months of the year. The site has a total of 2.8 million music tracks from which to choose. The combination of the popularity of tools that can play digital music and the availability of digital music on Web sites such as eMusic has made digital music the preferred mode for listening to music.

As discussed, digital music files contain information about the original analog sound that is encoded into binary digits made up of 0s and 1s, which represent the information about the original sound wave. These binary digits stand for specific frequencies and amplitudes of the original sound wave. Each digit needs to be converted back to the original frequency and amplitude for which it stands.

The first part of the process requires the conversion of the digital information into electrical signals that are sent to an audio amplifier. The amplifier then sends the electronic signals to a speaker, which converts the electrical information into sound waves. These are the sound waves that eventually make the listener's eardrums vibrate, making the sound audible. Since there are several steps in the process going from the binary information to sound waves, the primary challenge is avoiding loss of information so that there is little loss in sound quality.

The effects of loss is a matter of opinion and based on the kind of music that is being digitized. In 2004, *CNET* staff writer John Borland pointed out that, "Some very sharp sounds—a wood block, or a castanet recording—often wind up with what's called a 'pre-echo,' or a hint of the sound before the full instrument actually begins." Such losses could become irritating to those who are looking for a purer form of the music.

There are many reasons for loss of quality. For example, the digital file could be damaged and some of the sound information could have disappeared when the digital file was copied from one computer to another. Even though the copying process is supposed to take all the information from the original file and move it over to a new file, there could be a loss of information if there is an accidental interruption during copying. This could be caused by events such as a loss of power to the machine during the copying process.

Damage could also happen if there is a problem with the computer used to store the file. Sometimes there are tiny physical damages to a hard drive that can cause a loss of information, making the entire file unavailable for copying. Such situations would result in either a bad sound being produced or a complete loss of critical information about the original sound. The loss of information could make the sound file useless and the computer would not be able to decode the file at all.

Loss in quality could also happen when the electrical signals are sent to the amplifier. If the amplifier is not good, the electrical signals might be processed incorrectly, resulting in bad sound. Poor

Although headphones can give a user privacy because they prevent others from hearing what the user is listening to, using them at a high volume can result in temporary or permanent hearing loss. In 1983, headphone manufacturer Koss introduced the Safelite line of cassette players that warned the user when a dangerous volume was being used, but the line was discontinued after only two years due to lack of interest.

quality amplifiers are unable to handle all the different frequencies that make up a sound file. In such cases, the amplifier would not be able to accurately recreate the audio information encoded in the file.

Finally, if the speaker or the headphones are unable to correctly convert the electrical energy into sound waves, the sound might not be pleasing to the ear. This can happen with cheap headphones, which can distort the sound. This has led to the development of sophisticated headphones that can accurately recreate the original sound. Even with very good speakers and headphones, however, the most critical step is the conversion of the digital information into electrical signals, which needs to happen flawlessly to produce a pleasing listening experience.

DECODING DIGITAL SOUND FILES

As discussed in Chapter 2, the sound card is the key to the process of decoding digital audio and converting the digital information into electrical signals. The sound card is the hardware that is required to do the conversion. Several computer programs work with the sound card to do the computation required to convert binary data into electrical signals. "A good sound card is another part of the sound equation," writes John Blazevic of *PC Magazine*. "High-end speakers won't do you any good if you are using the built-in sound card." The sound card is the main connection between the computer and the speaker. A good sound card can significantly enhance the quality of the music.

The decoding process begins with the computer program that does the binary-to-decimal computation, taking each of the binary data points and converting it back to a specific part of the original wave. The entire analog wave is reproduced by combining all the wave information that is stored as binary data. Different kinds of decoding programs are able to handle a variety of sound formats. Each of the decoding programs is written to deal with different kinds of binary data. For example, the computer program offered by Apple Computers is designed to decode the files stored in the specific format used to encode sound in AAC. Even though there are different programs to decode different kinds of files, most of these programs are able to decode the standardized mp3 format.

The programs that decode the digital files do a series of calculations with the binary numbers. These calculations need to be done very rapidly since the electrical signals that are produced at the end of the calculations must be generated continuously to be sent to the speaker. Analog sound is heard as continuously produced sound waves that strike the eardrum. Any pauses in the sound waves would appear as silence, making it critical that the computer is able to convert the binary information into electrical signals without any interruptions. Otherwise, the sound would break up into small segments and the music would sound choppy.

The efficiency of the decoding process depends on how fast a computer can do the computations. Most computers are used for multiple purposes, and the process of decoding a digital audio file is just one of its many activities. The need for multitasking can lead to a slowing down of the decoding process, leading to a loss in the quality of the sound that is eventually produced. Loss in quality is avoided if the computer only decodes sound waves without having to do any other computations. This need has led to the development of specific gadgets that only decode binary sound files and do no other computations.

HEADPHONES

Headphones were first introduced in the 1930s and were used with radios during World War II. The first stereo headphones meant to be used for listening to music were developed in the United States by John C. Koss in 1958. Since then, many companies have developed headphones. There are several different kinds, such as earphones, earbuds, and the headset.

All headphones, no matter the style, have a small speaker that is placed close to the ear of the listener. The speaker is connected to an amplifier, which sends electrical signals that are converted to sound waves. Most headphones are only meant to be used to listen to sound, but some also have a microphone attached. These units are called headsets. They can be used both to convert electrical signals into sound waves and sound waves into electrical signals. The headset is often used with telephones when the user needs to listen and speak.

One of the strengths of headphones is their ability to operate with very weak electrical signals, since a very powerful amplifier is not required to produce sound waves using headphone speakers. This characteristic of headphones makes them suitable for gadgets that produce weak electrical signals, as is the case of portable music players. The electrical signal coming from a large amplifier is powerful enough to be sent to large speakers, but the electrical signal coming from a device such as an iPod would only be appropriate for headphones. The popularity of gadgets such as the iPod has brought headphones into high demand.

Another advantage of headphones is their portability. The size of headphones makes it easy to carry a pair without much difficulty. There has been a rapid development in headphone technology, leading to some that are remarkably small in size. Smaller headphones might be made up of a thin cable connected to tiny speakers that can fit comfortably in the ear. The speakers are pressed far into the ear canal, which requires very weak electrical energy to make the sound waves because the speakers are so close to the eardrum.

EQUIPMENT FOR DECODING SOUND FILES

There are many different kinds of equipment for playing digital sound files. The differences are in the format in which the sound information is stored and the kind of memory used to store the file. The traditional medium for storing digital sound has been the CD. Information on the CD is stored in the digital format called wave files, often containing the letters *wav* as the suffix of the file name. These files are usually large in size and only a limited number of files

(continues on page 64)

HEADPHONES

The most important aspect of headphones is the level of privacy they offer, since the sound made by their tiny speakers can only be heard by the person using the headphones. The sound is too soft to bother anyone else. Therefore, in public places such as airports, there could be thousands of people using personal digital music players without disturbing others around them. Headphones make it possible for each person to enjoy his or her personal music without bothering anyone.

People using headphones might not hear any sound other than what is coming from the speakers. The listener is cut off from the sound of the rest of the world and immersed in the audio space created by the headphones. This experience is accentuated even more by some headphones that come with noise cancellation tools that actively cut out any of the ambient noise. For example, people can use sound canceling headphones in an airplane to completely cut out the noise of the plane's engine, providing the listener with a soothing silence.

The disadvantage to noise-canceling headphones is that the listener would not be able to hear any surrounding sounds. Sometimes it is important to hear ambient sound. For example, in the United States there are numerous laws that make it illegal to drive a vehicle while wearing headphones. It is important that headphones are used carefully when it is necessary to listen to surrounding noises.

Headphone technology is constantly changing to provide good sound quality and better comfort, since many people use headphones for long hours. Headphones require a cable to connect them to the gadget that produces the sound waves, and there has been

(*opposite*) Headphones allow the listener to produce a personal sound space. Headphones can pick up the surrounding sounds, diminishing the quality of the listening experience. The noise-canceling headphone, however, is able to create electrical signals that cancel out the annoying sounds allowing the user to enjoy just the music.

ongoing research to eliminate the cable in order to make headphones more convenient to use. Emerging wireless technology allows the user to connect a transmitter to the source of music. For example, the Motorola S9 picks up the wire-

(continues)

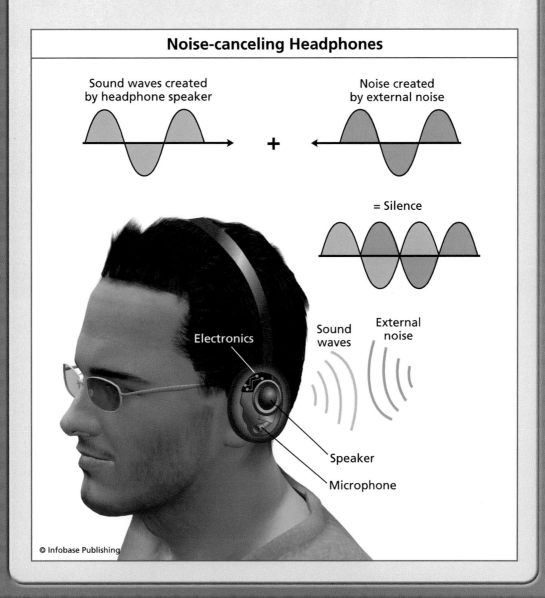

Noise-canceling Headphones

Sound waves created by headphone speaker

Noise created by external noise

+

= Silence

Electronics

Sound waves

External noise

Speaker

Microphone

© Infobase Publishing

(continued)

less signals sent by the transmitter connected to the music player and provides wireless access to music and voice calls. The user of such headphones can place the music player close to where the headphones are, without dealing with cumbersome cables. He or she can simply wear the headphones to enjoy the sound.

It is expected that headphones will become safer, smaller, and more comfortable, as suggested in a 2006 U.S. Patent Application from Sony Corporation for a set of headphones that would completely eliminate the need for wires by sending signals through the human body. The technology has been described by Adam Frucci of the online magazine *Gizmodo:* "The company is working on a technology to send music signals directly through your body. Because the signal is sent through a tiny electrostatic charge, they can only fit 48 kbps [kilobits per second, a unit of data transfer rate equal to 1,000 bits per second] into the transmission without it becoming a painful experience." It is quite possible that such technologies would become so commonplace that using headphones like these could become completely natural.

(continued from page 61)

can be stored on a CD. Playing these files requires equipment that can read the information that is written on the CD. A small laser beam travels across the face of the rotating disc in order to read the CD. The digital information read by the laser beam is deciphered using the electronic circuits of the CD player, which create the electrical signals that make a speaker or headphones vibrate to produce sound. The player can be used by itself or the CD player could be built into a computer to be used to read sound files as well as other digital files stored on a CD.

In 1982 Sony released the first CD player as one of the first gadgets able to decipher digital audio files. At the time, the CDP-101 sold in the United States for $900. Today, CD players can be installed in car audio systems, home stereo systems, and personal computers, and are also made as portable devices. The price tag for a portable CD player can be less than $20.

A desktop computer often has a CD player built into it. The sound card in the computer contains the electrical circuits to produce the electrical signals that are sent to the speakers. Manufacturers of desktop computers provide sophisticated speaker systems that can produce very high quality sound when connected to the computer. Digital sound files in many different formats can also be stored on the computer's hard drive. In this case, the sound files are stored on the hard drive just like all other files. The binary information is read off the hard drive and is then converted to electrical signals to be sent to the speakers. The computer can be a very versatile music player because it can use specific decoding software for specific sound file formats. The superior computing power of personal computers can be used to decode files of different formats, all of which can be converted to electrical signals. For example, a computer can decode the files stored on a CD as well as files in the mp3 format that are stored on its hard drive.

Both the CD player and computer-based digital file players require moving parts, making these tools more at risk for damage. For example, it is easy to damage the laser equipment in a CD player if it is accidentally dropped. The laser might also incorrectly read the file information in the case of sudden jolts. These players are also larger in size since they must have all the different parts that are needed to make them work properly. These disadvantages have led to the development of portable sound players that either do not require any moving parts or use very small moving parts. According to *CNET.com*, the advantages of the portable digital music player are that "they also have no moving parts, so their batteries last longer, and you can jog, snowboard, or bungee jump with them without causing skipping or damage." These advantages have helped to promote the use of portable digital music players.

Portable digital sound players decode digital sound files to produce electrical signals that can be sent to a pair of headphones. The two main components of the portable music player are the memory that is used to store the digital music files and the microprocessors that decode the digital information of the sound file. Although most portable sound players use similar microprocessors to decode digital information, there are two main ways in which the information is stored. One category of digital players depends on flash memory, as discussed in Chapter 3. These are usually smaller units that can store a maximum of five to six hours of music. These units also have small headphones, making the entire music unit quite small and portable.

The second category of digital music players uses tiny hard drives. These hard drives are designed only for music storage and reading. The use of the hard drive makes it possible to store far more files, so it is not uncommon to see portable players that can hold a very large number of songs. "The biggest advantage to a HDD [hard drive] player is the incredible amount of information you can store in a relatively small unit," writes Christopher Flowers of the online magazine *Top Ten Reviews.* "For example, the iPod video is just slightly larger than a deck of cards, yet it will store 60 gigabytes of data. This translates to 15,000 songs, 25,000 photographs or 150 hours of video."

An HDD player, also called an HD media player, is a product that combines a hard drive enclosure with hardware and software for playing audio, video, and photos. For instance, people with large collections of mp3 files that cannot be played on home stereo systems and a large collection of photographs stored on their digital cameras can use their HD media player to transfer or duplicate these files. The files can then be used in another location. The increased storage capacity can make these units much more desirable even if they could be somewhat bigger than the ones that use flash memory.

Most portable digital music players that are capable of storing large amounts of music files also provide a display screen with a set of buttons that allows the user to control the player. With thousands of files on a hard drive, the portable players need to provide a user-friendly interface that offers information about the files and

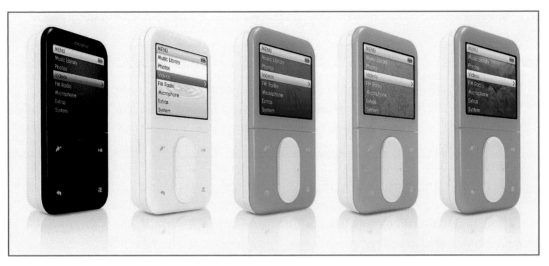

Since its launch in 2003, Apple has sold more than 220 million iPods worldwide, making it the best selling digital audio player series in history. Similar mp3 players (*above*) have also become popular as the technology continues to be more affordable.

simple controls to navigate through them. It is also possible to use the display to show digital video files that can be stored on the portable device. Some of the devices also allow for the storage of personal information such as phone numbers and schedules. These innovations are possible because of the rapid miniaturization of the storage system and the microprocessors needed to decode digital information. What began as simple mp3 players are now developing into small multipurpose devices.

It is important to note that a portable digital music player is typically only meant to decode digital music and is not able to encode analog sound into digital format. The memory devices in the player must be filled with the digital files before the player can be used. This means that the user must have a computer that can encode the music to place it on the player. If a user wants to frequently update the player's music content, it needs to be connected to a computer to complete the updates. Most players also come with accompanying encoding software that resides on the computer to which the player would be connected. For example, when one buys an iPod, the entire package

(continues on page 70)

iPOD®

According to Steven Levy in his 2006 book *The Perfect Thing: How the iPod Shuffles Commerce, Culture, and Coolness*, the iPod has created a new culture around the process of listening to music. The iPod is the name of a portable digital music player that was developed by Apple Computers and was first released in October 2001. By the end of 2006, between 7 million to 10 million iPods had been sold, beating all other players in customer popularity. Since the first iPod was released, 10 different iPod models have been developed. Additionally, the company releases limited numbers of special iPods, such as the red colored iPod that was released in 2006 to promote the fight against AIDS.

There are many reasons for the success of the iPod. Apple Computers spent a huge amount of money in advertising the iPod, targeting it for a young audience. The advertisements on many different media presented the iPod as a cool gadget, featuring the images of well-known popular musicians such as Bob Marley to go along with statements such as "iPod music is freedom." Apple Computers has a history of innovative advertising to sell its products and uses the world's best talents to market to technology-savvy and trendy customers.

In addition, the iPod is very user-friendly, requiring little technical knowledge since it has mechanized controls that most people can easily understand. Most iPods have a small screen where the user can see the list of songs stored on the machine and there is a touch sensitive control to navigate through the songs. Different iPods use either flash or hard drive technologies, so the smallest iPod models have the capacity to store several hundred songs and the largest iPods can store thousands of songs. The iPods that use a hard drive are also capable of recording video files that can then be viewed on the screen.

Although the term *iPod* has become synonymous with the portable mp3 player, there are other products similar to it. For example, companies such as Creative and Microsoft have popular digital music players. However, none of these products have had the cultural or economic impact of the iPod. According to BBC, "Digital music player maker Creative has seen a sharp fall in profits as it continues to battle with Apple's iPod for the lion's share of the market."

The various models appeal to different kinds of users. Those who want a tiny, stylish-looking gadget can get the smaller iPods in many different colors. Those who want to view video are able to buy iPods with built-in hard drives. The popularity of the iPod has given rise to a new set of products that can be used with the iPod. For example, the major fashion house Gucci has designed a $200 iPod carrying case.

Even though iPods are meant to be used by an individual wearing headphones, there is a large range of products that allow users to convert the iPod into a stereo. Portable speaker systems are available, as well as small adapters that can connect the iPod with a car's music system. Some car manufacturers have found ways to easily integrate the iPod into the development of their cars' audio systems. For example, BMW offers a connection to the iPod, as described in a 2004 news release from Apple: "The new system developed by Apple and BMW enables drivers to seamlessly use their iPod in BMW's 3 Series, Z4 Roadster, X3 and X5 Sports Activity Vehicles, and MINI Cooper by simply plugging their iPod into a cable located in the car's glove compartment." With these integrated systems, the driver uses the controls of the car's music system to select music from the iPod and to listen through the car's speakers.

In 2007 Apple Computers released a new product called the iPhone, which combined the capabilities of an iPod with a cell phone. Within 74 days of its release, one million units had been sold in the United States. Much like the original iPod, the phone was meant for people who were more interested in creating a culture and fashion statement. Many critics, such as Edward F. Moltzen, who writes for the technology magazine *CRN*, have suggested that the iPhone is not the best cellular phone. Nevertheless, the appeal of the iPod transferred to the iPhone. Like the iPod, the iPhone offers many user-friendly options such as its touch-sensitive screen that acts as the phone keyboard, an Internet browser, and a video viewer. The novelty and the ease of use of the iPhone made it an instant favorite among those who were already happy with the iPod.

(continued from page 67)

includes the computer program, iTunes, required to run the iPod. When using such computer programs, the portable digital music player needs a paired computer that feeds the files to the player.

These devices have led to increased customization of music consumption, since people can now carry their favorite music with them. They are able to listen to the music of their own choice rather than a pre-packaged radio program or what is put on music CDs. This versatility has created a condition in which people can completely customize the music they are listening to, making the computer and the portable music player into personalized jukeboxes.

A COMPUTER AS A JUKEBOX

Music digitization has made it possible for listeners to customize the music they listen to, much in the way a traditional jukebox works. A jukebox holds numerous vinyl albums, cassette tapes, or CDs, allowing users to listen to personally selected music. In the case of mechanical jukeboxes, the machine physically moves the CD to the correct place to play from a specific point in the CD. The technology is bulky because of the large storage space required for numerous media, and these machines are not meant for personal use. They are often found in restaurants and bars.

Until recently, music has almost always been packaged in bundles, with bands releasing CDs that contain several songs. Listeners have been obligated to buy the complete CD, even if they wanted to listen to only a couple of favorite songs. When it comes to radio stations, specific lists of songs are selected to be played during a certain time frame, accompanied by commercials. For an hour-long popular music program, music from different artists provides the radio listener with a large degree of variety in the music. Before digitization, it was difficult to listen to particular songs from different groups because listeners had to constantly change CDs to set up the desired sequence.

With the digital music player, the listener can select which songs to listen to in which sequence. Digitization converts each separate piece of music, such as a specific song, into a unique digital file. For example, digitizing 10 songs from a CD would produce 10 different digital files, each having a different file name. Music players also use computer programs to catalog the files with special identification tags. Using these tags, users are able to search for specific pieces of music in order to play them in customized sequences. Any combination of such files can later be played in any order chosen by the user. Files from different sources can be combined and placed next to each other to create a specific list to be played, called a playlist. It's the digital equivalent of a portable jukebox within every user's reach. The digital jukebox can then be connected with the traditional music player to create a customized, high-quality audio experience. The process of digitization offers freedom to the listener by giving him or her the ability to choose what he or she would like to listen to.

SYNTHESIZING THE COMPUTER AND TRADITIONAL SOUND PLAYER

Personal digital music players usually operate with headphones that provide a musical experience to one person and make it difficult to share the music. The portable digital music player is usually not

Pictured is an amplifier, or amp. The amplifier makes sounds louder, depending on how high a wave (or energy) is. The higher the wave, the louder the sound.

HOME DIGITAL AUDIO

Digital music can be integrated with other audio systems, with the most popular integration being between the audio amplifier and the computer. The marriage between these two tools is especially interesting because the computer deals with binary information whereas the audio amplifier has traditionally been analog equipment. The increasing digitization of sound has led to a change in audio amplifier technology, with some audio amplifiers also acting as DACs. Thus, the amplifier will accept digital data from the computer and convert it into analog electrical signals to be sent to the speakers.

The process does not use the microprocessor in the computer to do any digital to analog conversion, but instead turns that task over to the amplifier. The advantage of this process lies in the fact that the microprocessor in the amplifier is usually designed to deal specifically with audio data, whereas the microprocessor is designed for many different tasks. This makes the microprocessor better suited for sound-related computations, producing a higher sound quality.

When music is stored as digital files on the hard drive of a computer, the user must have a way of easily accessing the files to listen to the music using the audio ampli-

powerful enough to be connected to large speakers, and the quality of the sound is good only when listened to on the headphones. On the other hand, a computer offers a better quality of sound when speakers are connected to the computer's sound card. Still, even the computer does not have a powerful enough amplifier that can make the analog sound rich, powerful, and loud.

The sound card in the computer can also be used to connect the computer to an audio amplifier with special connectors that go between the computer and the amplifier. The electrical signal coming from the computer is boosted by the amplifier and sent to the more powerful speakers that are connected to the amplifier,

fier. Many users have thousands of music files on their computers. This requires simple ways of controlling the computer when connecting it to the audio amplifier, with the computer, keyboard, and mouse being close to the audio amplifier. The placement may pose a challenge because the computer with its monitor and other attachments might not look good placed next to an amplifier. To solve this problem, many computer manufacturers provide wireless connections between the computer and the amplifier, so the two gadgets now do not need to be next to each other. Instead, the digital files travel from the computer to the amplifier over radio waves.

The large numbers of digital music files that are on the hard drive of an average user's computer also need to be efficiently cataloged for easy searching. Computers automatically retrieve file information (song title, artist, genre, etc.) from CDs when the user inputs them. Yahoo, for one, provides an appropriately named computer program called Jukebox, which creates and shares music playlists. One of the ways of doing this is to build playlists made up of sequences of music that the user chooses. For instance, a user might create a playlist of all piano music, and then a listener would simply select the list and listen to the various piano tunes that are included in the playlist. Building a playlist is one of the best ways to customize the music that is played on the audio amplifier.

producing a richer sound. The ability to connect a computer to a traditional audio amplifier is leading to an increasing integration of the computer into music systems. Many users are now placing their music players next to their computers so that they can be conveniently connected.

The need to connect a computer to a music system has emerged from the desire to get the best quality sound from a computer. These gadgets bypass the sound card, producing a better quality sound by using the unused capabilities of the main microprocessor of the computer. These main microprocessors are getting increasingly more powerful, allowing for efficient processing of digital sound files and making the computer an integral part of the way in which people listen to music. "Playing digital music through your home audio system is a logical extension of playing the same digital audio files on your computer," writes Michael Miller in *InformIT*. This is becoming increasingly popular as companies such as Hewlett Packard are selling computers built specifically to connect with the user's home audio system.

The computer can also be connected to the Internet, which can be used to send compressed digital music files from one person to another. At the same time, a computer connected to both the Internet and an audio amplifier can play sound files that are available on the Internet.

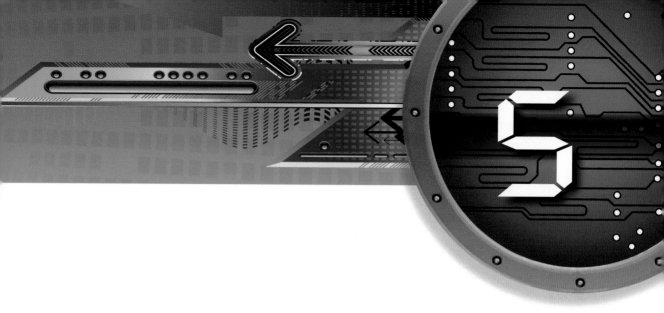

Sounds on the Internet

A large amount of legal and illegal exchanges of music has been made possible by the digitization of music into compressed binary files that can easily be exchanged over the Internet using networked computers. In 2006 a total of one billion pieces of music were sold by the Internet music store iTunes, owned by Apple Computers. This followed the first popular surge of downloading music in 2000, when nearly 6 million people were involved in the illegal sharing of music between individuals using a system called Napster. This chapter looks at some of the key technological issues related to the way in which music files are exchanged, and then examines the primary consequences of sharing digital music files. This chapter also describes the way in which the Internet itself has been enhanced by using digitized music as part of the material available online.

It is first useful to consider the key components of the Internet, which is built around thousands of nodal computers that are owned by different institutions. (A node is any device connected to a computer network. This can be computers, personal digital assistants, cell phones, or various other technological appliances.) For example, nearly every university in the United States is an Internet node that represents powerful computers that are connected to other nodes. The connections among the nodes can carry data at extremely high speeds. Personal computers belonging to individuals are also connected to these nodes. For example, a university student would connect his or her personal computer to the university node and quickly access the global network. Most personal computers in developed countries can use fast broadband data connections to communicate with the nodal machines. With millions of people continuously using the Internet, the connected computers are constantly exchanging binary data with one another. The large flow of information is creating the need for data compression so that the data can be rapidly exchanged. These issues impact the way in which music is digitized for the Internet.

It is necessary to make sure that the digitization process produces a small file that would easily travel over the Internet. The mp3 format is suitable for this purpose because this format provides a balance between sound quality and file size. Once an mp3 file reaches a networked computer, it can be stored on the hard drive of the computer for future use without an Internet connection. For example, a user can receive an e-mail message with an mp3 file attached to it, which can then become a part of the library of mp3 music files on the user's computer. The mp3 file can then also be moved between computers or to a portable digital music player, which would not need an Internet connection to play the music file. In this situation, the Internet becomes the medium used to transport digital music files from one point to another, just like a music CD can be sent from one person to another through postal mail.

With the growth of the popularity of music digitization, there is also a demand to have music coming into a networked computer for real-time listening. In this case, the file would not be stored on the computer; instead, the user would listen to the music as it is downloaded from a nodal computer. When music is exchanged in this way, the file has to be delivered in a format that is small in size and suitable for any computer connected to the Internet. The file also needs to be transferred over high-speed computer connections so that there are no delays and the sound can be heard uninterrupted.

These files are decoded by special computer programs called media players, which use shared libraries and are designed to rapidly interpret the digital content of files. For example, the Windows operating system has a built-in media player called Windows Media Player, which is used for playing audio and video, as well as for viewing images on computers running the Windows system. The music is usually delivered in a format specific to the computer program that would be used to decode the music file, and the user is able to obtain the decoding programs free of cost from different Web sites. Apple's Mac OS X comes pre-loaded with another media player called QuickTime, used to play QuickTime movies, in addition to iTunes for playing a variety of media formats. Examples of media players that use media libraries are Winamp, Windows Media Player, iTunes, RealPlayer, Amarok, and ALLPlayer.

Thus, there are two main ways of delivering sounds over the Internet: Either the file would be downloaded for storage or the file would be sent over a high-speed network for playback in real time. Of these two methods, real-time playback has gained popularity as suggested by the fact that in early 2007 there were nearly 72 million monthly listeners of Internet radio.

REAL-TIME DELIVERY OF DIGITAL AUDIO FILES

Users of the Internet are accustomed to accessing information that resides on other computers connected to the Internet without necessarily having to permanently download the files to their own machines. When Web-based information is used on a computer, the digital material is stored as a temporary file that is deleted once the user moves away to a new Web site. Many users are interested in applying the same strategy to digital music to be able to simply listen to music online without permanently storing it in the memory of their personal machines. Users want the files coming into their computers to be decoded as music, without having to clutter the hard drive with too many files.

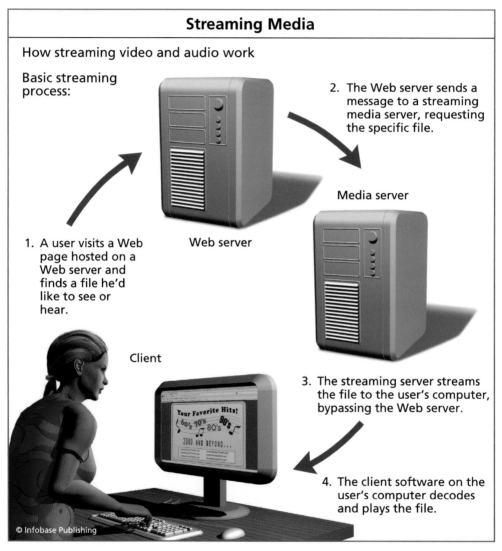

Streaming Media

How streaming video and audio work

Basic streaming process:

1. A user visits a Web page hosted on a Web server and finds a file he'd like to see or hear.

Web server

2. The Web server sends a message to a streaming media server, requesting the specific file.

Media server

Client

3. The streaming server streams the file to the user's computer, bypassing the Web server.

4. The client software on the user's computer decodes and plays the file.

© Infobase Publishing

Streaming media refers to a digital audio or video file that is sent to a computer from a media server that holds numerous digital audio or video files. Usually the user or client's computer would have a connection to the Internet that allows for rapid transfer of files, and the client is then able to use the personal computer to decode the digital audio and video information to enjoy the content that is sent out by the media server.

The trend has become popular, as described by *PC World Magazine:* "[Streaming audio is] a technology that lets you listen to music and other types of sound files in real time over the Internet without lengthy downloads." The most important aspect of this form of music file delivery is that the files on the central nodal computer can be constantly updated, allowing users access to a much larger set of files than what the hard drive of a single personal computer can store.

The process of streaming involves downloading a sound file to a temporary memory area of the computer called the buffer. The computer that is used to listen to the music remains connected to the Internet to download the digital audio file and store it in the buffer. Each of the downloaded sections is decoded using the digital to analog converter and associated computer program of the user's machine. It is thus converted into audible sound. While the conversion is going on, the buffer area is refilled with another portion of the sound file, which is likewise converted to sound. This allows the listener to hear uninterrupted sound.

The popularity of streaming files has made it important for computers to have buffers large enough to store the amount of data that comes in from the nodal computer. This is particularly true if there is a slow connection between the computer that plays the music and the nodal computer that stores the music files. For example, if someone is connected to the Internet using phone lines, faulty or old lines could slow down the delivery of the file so that some parts are delayed. Such interruptions in the stream create pauses between different parts of the audio. The user needs to ensure that there is a sufficiently large buffer that allows for the storage of the downloaded files, because a larger buffer would ensure that there would be fewer moments of silence.

At the same time, there also needs to be some degree of balance between the size of the buffer and how fast the computer can decode the digital audio information into electrical signals. If too much of the computer memory is used as a buffer, the computer loses its computing capabilities and cannot perform the computations required for decoding the file.

There are many different issues involved in sending streaming audio files over the Internet, so there needs to be a connection between the different technological components to ensure that there is an efficient flow of audio files. Among all these issues, the most important concern is the speed at which files can travel over the Internet. Better connections using methods such as fiber-optic lines are increasing the speed at which data can be sent from one computer to another. The success achieved in increasing the speed at which data travels is making real-time audio streaming popular. Many different Web sites now use streaming audio as a standard part of the material they make available online. For example, the Web site for the news service CNN has a separate section called CNN Radio that provides streaming audio news.

ONLINE RADIO SERVICES

Radio is a medium where messages are not usually stored. Instead, signals go from the radio station to the listener. Radio broadcasts are done in real time with little expectation that the broadcasts will be saved or stored. Programs could be recorded by the listener, but most radio programs are lost forever after they have been broadcast. Radio is a very local medium, particularly the type of radio waves that use frequency modulation (FM) to send high-quality audio signals. FM transmission cannot travel very long distances, so most radio stations have to operate within a small geographic area.

The combination of streaming audio and the global reach of the Internet offers the opportunity for local radio stations to have a global presence. Audio streaming on the Internet is called webcasting since it does not travel over wires. Like traditional radio, webcasting presents listeners with a steady stream of audio that cannot be replayed or paused. This makes Internet radio different from on-demand file serving and podcasting, which require the listener to download and store files.

The trend of streaming radio programs began with a few pioneering radio stations. For example, in 1994, WXYC in Chapel

Hill, North Carolina, began to put its radio signals on the Internet. That same year, the rock group the Rolling Stones was the first to have a "major cyberspace multicast concert." Lead singer Mick Jagger opened the concert by saying, "I wanna say a special welcome to everyone that's, uh, climbed into the Internet tonight and, uh, has got into the M-bone [experimental multicast backbone]. And I hope it doesn't all collapse." In March 1996, London's Virgin Radio became the first European radio station to broadcast live on the Internet 24 hours a day. Internet broadcasting began to attract investors and lots of attention from other media. These pioneering Internet broadcasters were followed by thousands of radio stations across the globe.

Some traditional radio broadcasting institutions such as the British Broadcasting Corporation (BBC) and America's National Public Radio (NPR) stream the same audio programs from their radio broadcasts. These radio stations did not produce any special content for the Internet component of the radio broadcast, but rather used the Internet as a supplement to the primary business of broadcast radio.

There are also radio stations that exist only on the Internet, without any presence as a traditional radio station. These stations came into existence because of the development of streaming audio and are often operated by small organizations. For example, one of the most popular Internet radio stations, Pandora, is based on the Music Genome Project, which categorizes music in special ways so that listeners can find the exact match for the music they might want to hear. "Each song in the Music Genome Project is analyzed using up to 400 distinct musical characteristics by a trained music analyst," explains the Pandora Web site. "These attributes capture not only the musical identity of a song, but also the many significant qualities that are relevant to understanding the musical preferences of listeners." There are other groups like Pandora that put up very specialized kinds of Internet radio programs.

Internet broadcasts make radio stations available as long as there is an Internet connection, eliminating the problem of geographic restrictions to broadcasting radio signals. Most traditional radio stations already had good audio equipment when webcasting technology came about, so they only had to digitize the audio signal to be sent out as digital files using computers connected to the Internet. A listener can access radio stations from anywhere in the world. For example, someone in Europe is able to listen to a station in Australia, making Internet radio very popular with people who leave their home countries to live somewhere else.

Today it is safe to say that there are several thousand Internet radio stations. As with traditional radio stations, they focus on different categories. There are Internet radio stations for children and teens that play mostly popular music and offer information about teen-related issues. There are news-oriented stations that deliver local and worldwide news. There are stations that discuss various informational topics such as cooking and gardening. Usually these stations allow listeners to call in and have their say about the topic. Sports radio stations provide listeners with the results of important games and sometimes offer interviews. Religious radio stations offer listeners religious text readings, talkback radio discussions, and music. There are even teaching radio stations through which children in remote areas of the world receive their education. With educational Internet radio stations, lessons can be followed and broadcasts can reach large groups at the same time.

PERFORMANCE ROYALTIES

In 1998, the U.S. Congress passed the Digital Millennium Copyright Act, which states that performance royalties are to be paid for satellite radio (radio broadcast using communications satellite signals) and Internet radio broadcasts, in addition to publishing royalties. With traditional radio broadcasts, only publishing royalties are paid. As a result, SaveNetRadio.org was created by a coalition of listeners, artists, labels, and webcasters who criticized the proposed royalty rates, saying that these rates were burdensome to independent, Internet-only stations and smaller stations. An August 2008

Washington Post article reported that Pandora, one of the nation's most popular Web radio services with its one million daily listeners, was on the verge of collapse due to performance royalty payments for webcasters. In January 2009, the U.S. Copyright Board announced that it will provide performance royalty to streaming net services based on revenue.

Even with the ongoing performance royalty dispute, as of 2007, according to Bridge Ratings and Research, "there were some 57 million weekly listeners of Internet radio programs. More people listen to online radio than to satellite radio, high-definition radio, podcasts, or cell-phone-based radio combined." A 2008 survey showed that more than 1 in 7 persons in the United States aged 25 to 54 listen to Internet radio each week.

ONLINE MUSIC SERVICES

The process of obtaining music files from computers connected to the Internet uses the same principle as Internet radio stations: A digital audio file is placed on a nodal computer and the file can then be transferred to a personal computer connected to the Internet. Numerous Web sites and Internet resources make music files available to anyone with access to the nodal computer. The success of this process depends on the kind of nodal computer that is available. A good nodal machine has a fast connection to the Internet and has a large hard drive to store many different audio files. These two requirements lead to a demand for very expensive computers that can serve the needs of thousands of people who could be simultaneously trying to access files on the nodal machine.

The technological demands produced by the process of obtaining files from one central computer was partly resolved with the development of a feature called peer-to-peer (P2P) file sharing. The process was first developed in 1999 by an Irish computer scientist named Ian Clarke who, while completing his final project at college, developed the first P2P system called the Freenet Project. Freenet pools the contributed bandwidth and storage space of member computers and allows users to anonymously publish or retrieve various types of information. It offers strong protection of freedom of speech and is free and open to all users. Freenet attracted media attention and became the seed for future P2P systems.

The P2P process reduced the importance of the nodal computer since the digitized file could now remain on the hard drive of any computer connected to the Internet. Special computer programs would connect any computer to similar computers all over the Internet, allowing access to a huge virtual library of files. Any of these files could be copied from one machine to another as long as they both were connected to the Internet. The P2P process removed the need for a central depository of files and instead made a giant list of files accessible through the P2P network.

The company that pioneered the use of P2P technology for exchanging digital music files was called Napster, which developed a simple computer program that allowed people to connect to a global P2P network. Its creators, university student Shawn Fanning and his friend Sean Parker, developed the service as an easier way to find music without searching web portals such as Lycos. The Napster system allowed people to share mp3 files with other users, bypassing music industry

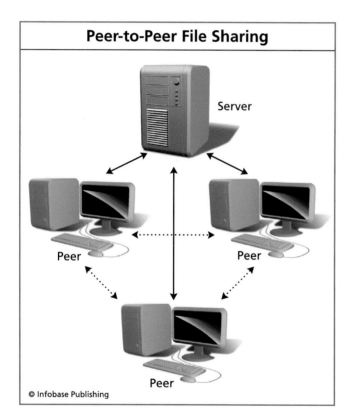

Peer-to-Peer File Sharing

Server

Peer

Peer

Peer

© Infobase Publishing

A significant amount of digital information is shared between individual computers through the process of peer-to-peer file sharing. Each computer in the network connects to a server over the Internet and each computer or peer can access the files on the other computer or peer. This technology is used for sharing music, as in the case of Napster.

Shawn Fanning (*right*), the founder of Napster, created a code for a program to make downloading music easier by allowing users to bypass the usual channels for songs. Fanning launched Napster in 1999, and it quickly became one of the most popular ways to download songs. Although Napster was shut down by court order in 2001, it paved the way for decentralized peer-to-peer file-sharing programs.

companies and other established markets for these songs. Napster, during its operation from 1999 until 2001, provided the computer program for free and never had a way to make any money for itself.

What it did do was bring about a revolution in the way online music would be used by millions of listeners. "Napster inventor Shawn Fanning spent the past year presiding over the end of the world as we know it," wrote Rob Sheffield in *Rolling Stone* magazine in 2000. "His pioneering mp3 sharing technology changed the way fans discover, explore, and enjoy music." At its peak, it had nearly 26.4 million people using its service worldwide, but drew strong opposition from the record industry and some musicians. In 2000, rock band Metallica filed a lawsuit against Napster after discovering that a demo of its song "I Disappear" had been circulating the network, even before its release. This resulted in the song being played on several radio stations. A month later, rapper Dr. Dre filed a similar suit after Napster refused to remove his works from the service, despite a written request. Later that year, several record companies sued Napster for copyright infringement. In 2001, a district court ruled against Napster and the company shut down its services.

THE PEER-TO-PEER DEBATE

Peer-to-peer (P2P) file-sharing networks have grown to serve millions of users. With their increase in popularity, these networks have also become a target for users to spread malware (software designed to damage a computer) through file-sharing applications. In addition, copyright holders and publishers have stated that the unauthorized downloading of multimedia has damaged the economy. Others have said that the decline in sales cannot be blamed on file sharing.

It is actually difficult to determine blame. In 1999, the year of Napster's launch, sales of recorded music were $38.5 billion. A report from Enders Analysis predicts overall sales for 2009 to be $23 billion, which is a significant decrease. According to Claire Enders, the blame falls on the "adoption of digital technology that is eating the industry alive, and it's taken a number of different forms, in particular, piracy, copying of music, creating compilations for oneself, or handing them around to one's friends." This adoption is said to have led to the closing of Tower Records, a retail music store, and the release of two profit warnings from entertainment retail store HMV.

Nonetheless, there are plenty of advocates for file sharing. For one, file sharing is not always illegal and sharing helps the affected industry by allowing the consumer to sample

Although Napster was shut down, it paved the way for decentralized P2P file-sharing networks. File sharing provides access to digitally stored information, including computer programs, multimedia such as movies and music, documents, and electronic books. File-sharing networks have also been accused of copyright infringement, and many services have shut down due to lawsuits by groups such as the Record Industry Association of America and the Motion Picture Association of America.

the product before buying, according to supporters. This helps sales because the consumer can sample a lower-quality version or one song from a CD before buying it, whereas he or she might never buy a full CD without being able to hear a sample on the computer first. Supporters also argue that CDs are far too expensive relative to their cost of production, and if a consumer only wants one or two songs, he or she should not be forced to buy an entire CD. Others suggest that access to creative works such as music and film is a right and should not be controlled by distributors. Finally, there is the argument that P2P file sharing is only one possible cause of the decrease in CD sales since other types of media that have file sharing—gaming, movies—have seen a rise, not a drop in sales.

Whatever side is taken, file sharing is here to stay. According to a 2008 *Los Angeles Times* survey on U.S. campuses, 64 percent of respondents download music regularly through file-sharing networks and other unauthorized sources. When asked on a scale of 1 to 7 (1 meaning not concerned, 7 meaning extremely concerned) how nervous they were about being punished for illegal downloading, two-thirds answered 1 or 2, with none giving a 7. This attitude is global. According to a 2009 Tiscali survey done in Sweden, 75 percent of young voters supported file sharing when presented with the statement, "I think it is OK to download files from the Net, even if it is illegal."

BUYING MUSIC

As discussed in Chapter 4, online purchasing of digitized music has become a very large global business. The popularity of online music sales is partly related to problems with the traditional way of selling music. For example, a music CD that sells for $20 could contain 12 to 14 songs but only have a couple of songs that appeal to the consumer. Still, the consumer would have to pay the full amount for the CD. In the past, popular singles were released as vinyl albums containing only two songs—one on each side of the disc. They were released to radio stations, which created playlists by stacking single albums against each other to create a customized list of songs. The possibility of digitizing music has led to an interest in going back to customized playlists, where consumers can combine their favorite songs while leaving out the songs they don't like.

These demands led to the development of many different kinds of online music stores, such as the iTunes Store owned by Apple Computers. The iTunes Store is accessed either through a Web site or by using a small program residing on a computer that is connected to the Internet. The store offers thousands of single pieces of music that can be purchased for as little as 99 cents each. The store has made arrangements with music distributors to allow iTunes users to download music from the iTunes Store to be transferred to an iPod. In the case of the iTunes Store, the music is sold in a format that can only be played on the iPod and payments can be made by using standard credit cards. Once users set up accounts with the iTunes Store, they can purchase as much music as they want. With reported revenues of $808 million in 2008, iTunes has enjoyed record sales of its music.

Other, similar stores have also become popular, with eMusic rising as a competitor to iTunes. The eMusic store has a smaller collection of music to choose from but the music is sold in the universal mp3 format, making it possible to play the purchased music on virtually any kind of digital music player. What is important to note about online trading in music is that stores like iTunes only sell binary data and this data must be stored on a hard drive for the customer to listen to the music. With music purchased online, the purchase will be useless if the data gets damaged due to a fault with the hard drive, unlike with CDs bought at a physical store.

There are other Internet-based stores that sell streaming music. As previously mentioned, streaming music is not stored on the computer; instead, with these online stores, users pay a periodic fee to be able to stream digital audio files through a Web site. These companies often provide a free computer program that simplifies the streaming process. For example, the company Live365 allows the user to download a program that remains on the user's computer that allows access to a large amount of streaming audio files that are played on the computer in realtime. These stores give users a vast range of online, real-time music to choose from but do not allow a user to download the files onto his or her computer. These services only work when the computer is connected to the Internet. It is very similar to the way in which Internet radio stations work, except that the user must listen to commercials in between songs or pay a fee to listen to the music available at these stores, while many radio stations provide content for free.

Like iTunes, stores selling online music subscriptions do not sell anything you can actually hold. The user only gains the right to access a library of music. As long as the computer is connected to the Internet, the user is able to access the music.

PODCASTING

Pew Internet Research reported in 2006 that nearly 17 million American adults had listened to podcasts that year. A podcast is a pre-recorded audio program that is posted to a Web site and made available for download so that people can listen to it on their personal computer or mobile device. The audio broadcast has been converted to an mp3 file or other type of audio file format to be played at the listener's convenience.

Podcasts are appealing because they are often free, they allow people to customize a mix of programs from millions of Web sites, they are available for listening or viewing at any time on a

CREATING A PODCAST

According to Pew Internet Research, there has been an increase in the number of people making podcasts, as well as an increase in the number of podcast listeners. Making podcasts is appealing to podcasters because of its user-friendliness, and it is a way to get a message out to a large global audience for very little money. Podcasts are appealing to listeners because they are often free, they allow people to customize the programs they want to listen to, they are available for listening or viewing at any time on a computer or portable playback device, and the listener does not have to review hundreds of Web sites to find new programs.

In order to create a podcast, one needs to start with three items: a microphone, a computer, and Internet access. Once you have these items, there are four basic steps:

1) **Plan.** Before getting your voice on audio, it is impor-tant to know what infor-mation you are trying to convey. If you stay focused, in the end you will pro-duce a better podcast and gain more listeners. Take the time to consider your topic, the format, and the location of your podcast.

2) **Produce.** Once you have written your notes, you can create your audio file. Most Windows-based computers come with sound-recording software built in. On the Windows XP system, you can find it by going to Start > All Programs > Accessories > Entertainment > Sound Recorder. You can use this tool to play around with the microphone that came with your computer or one that plugs into it. You can also use a com-puter program such as

computer or portable playback device, and they save time because users no longer have to check hundreds of Web sites to find out what's new. Podcasts also offer subscription services, meaning

Audacity, which includes a tool to edit the sound file. It is best to record and save your file in .wav format until you have done all of the editing you want. That will give you a master file to work from and a backup in case there is a problem. Then, export the file to mp3 format for distribution. If you want to play music, you will need to set it up as a stereo file.

3) **Publish your podcast.** Now, upload your audio file to the Internet. This involves creating an mp3 file, naming your podcast file, uploading your podcast, writing your podcast show notes, and posting your show notes. You can publish your podcast by registering for a Web site, also called a domain name; by buying a Web host, which stores your blog or Web site and your audio files on the Internet; by starting a blog, which is your Web site for posting your show notes, links, etc.; or by creating an RSS feed, which is the feed that your listeners will subscribe to in order to automatically download episodes of your podcast.

4) **Promote your podcast.** The podcaster can promote his or her podcast by advertising it on various Web sites, including his or her own blog. For example, there are several Web-based services that provide directions for promoting a podcast, such as podcastfreeamerica.com.

For more detailed, step-by-step instructions on how to create your own podcast, please see http://www.how-to-podcast-tutorial.com/00-podcast-tutorial-four-ps.htm.

users can receive new files from a particular program automatically by subscription.

Examples of podcast subscription servers are iTunes, MyYahoo, and RSS (short for Really Simple Syndication). The servers will check the user's feeds regularly for new works. The receiver of the podcast can browse through many lists of audio files to pick out the podcasts that appear interesting. For example, the podcast service called podcastdirectory.com offers the visitor a series of categories of podcasts from which to choose, ranging from podcasts related to comedy to those dealing with religion and spirituality. The selected digital file can then be downloaded from the central Internet storage to the listener's computer. The listener can then listen to the podcast at a convenient time. "It makes delivering content to listeners simple and convenient, while new technology has made creating them easier than ever before," wrote Curtis Robinson in the *Atlanta Tribune* in 2006. Podcasting has become popular primarily because it is a fairly simple technology and computers are sophisticated enough that it requires very little technological expertise to create a podcast.

Although podcasting takes its name from Apple's iPod, it isn't limited only to iPod users. As long as a listener has a computer, which is to say the vast majority of podcast users, then there is no need for special software. What is needed is the audio player that comes with the computer, such as Windows Media Player or RealPlayer. For those who wish to subscribe to a podcast feed, it is necessary to install podcatcher software, such as iTunes or Juice.

The popularity of podcasts has created a demand for music to use on the shows for low expense and little licensing difficulty. As a result, a growing number of songs by independent as well as established musicians have been designated as "podsafe." The implications of podcasting are quite profound because this technology is changing the relationship between communication and power. Before podcasting became popular, it was necessary to have a certain degree of power to be able to communicate to a large audience. For example, radio stations need significant financial power to operate; even a small radio station requires an annual budget of about a million dollars. It is usually not possible for just anyone to set up a radio station with a global audience. Podcasts have changed this relationship because now anyone who is willing to learn how to do a podcast can gain a voice on the Internet. It does not require lots of money or equipment to be able to make a podcast, giving a sense of power to an individual.

One can become a podcaster using four free tools: Blogger, a blog-based Web site where you can post information about your shows and blog about any topic; audio software such as Audacity with the Lame plug-in, which is free audio recording and editing software; set up a Web site using a service such as Internet Archive, which provides free hosting and bandwidth; and FeedBurner, a free service for hosting your RSS feed.

Because nearly anyone can produce a podcast, it also puts more responsibility on the listener to be critical of what he or she chooses to hear. Institutional voices of radio were seen as more trustworthy because the listener assumed that the institutions were careful about the quality of what was being broadcast. For example, the BBC has numerous editors who review a story before it is broadcast, ensuring that the news is reliable and properly presented. There is no such system in place for podcasters because there are no overseers as there are with mainstream media outlets.

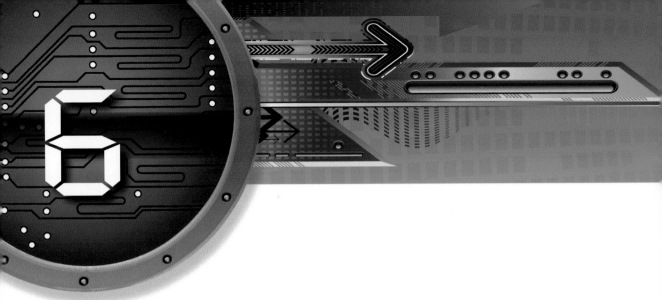

Protecting Digital Sound

The digitization of sound has allowed for the production of digital files that can be easily moved from one computer to another or from a computer to a portable digital music player. Digital files created in the mp3 format can be played on virtually any digital device and the files are small enough to be sent from one computer to another using the Internet. The Internet, too, has become a fast network, as computers are able to connect to one another over connections that can rapidly carry large amounts of binary data. The combination of these factors has made it very simple to share digital audio files among different computers.

The ease with which files can be exchanged has led to a set of concerns about the ethics of sharing files, especially when anyone with a computer can trade in digital music. The uncontrolled exchange of files, which has been described as stealing music, can become very damaging for people who are connected with the music industry. According to the Recording Industry Association of America

(RIAA), "Across the board, this theft has hurt the music community, with thousands of layoffs, songwriters out of work, and new artists having a harder time getting signed and breaking into the business."

Unlike the CD, which you can carry with you from place to place, digitized music does not have a physical existence on the Internet. Even though the surface of the CD contains digital information, a user must have the actual CD to access its files. In the case of the Internet, the digital file made up of binary digits remains as specific alignments of magnetic information on the hard drive

Compact discs (CDs) were originally created to store sound exclusively, but today they also are used for storing all types of data, including videos, photographs, and text.

of a computer. These digits can be sent as electrical signals over a wire in the same way that an e-mail travels from one computer to another. No physical object needs to be moved from one computer to another. This makes it much easier to send music over distances, as long as the sender and the receiver are connected to the same network, such as the Internet.

If computers are not connected to a reliable network, music files can still be shared by copying the files into a portable medium

TYPES OF CDS

Before using a CD, it is important to know what kind you need. Data CDs are used to store files and folders, such as those on your hard drive. Although these CDs can be played in computers that have a CD-ROM or CD-Recorder, they cannot be played in your car or home stereo. Audio CDs are used to record music from tracks and audio files, such as .wav or mp3 files. Unlike data CDs, audio CDs can be played on a stereo.

There are two types of audio CDs: CD-Recordable (CD-R) and CD-ReWritable (CD-RW). CD-Rs can be used in all CD-ROMs and other drives, whereas CD-RW can only be used in CD-RW drives or newer multiread CD-ROMs. CD-Rs can be used in stereos, are less expensive than CD-RWs, and are excellent for permanent data storage. The one drawback is that once data has been recorded onto the CD-R, it cannot be erased.

CD-RWs cost more (because of the 3 percent performance royalty paid to the music industry for making the copy) and cannot be used in a stereo made prior to 1997. They can, however, be recorded over and over, roughly up to 1,000 times, which can save you money in the long run. It is best to use a CD-RW to make practice CDs or to test the content of a CD before making a permanent one. CD-RWs never gained the popularity of the CD-Rs due to their higher price, lower recording and reading speeds, and compatibility issues with CD reading units.

such as the CD. Interestingly, the technology for creating CDs has been available since 1976, but it was only in the late 1990s that the equipment became affordable to a regular computer user. This was coupled with the availability of the writable CD, called a recordable compact disc or CD-R, which records compressed digital audio files and can be used with most personal computers. By 2003, nearly 140 million people owned the technology to create their own CDs and nearly 60 percent of them actually used this technology. A CD containing compressed digital audio files could be used to make multiple copies of the files for distribution.

As long as all parts of the binary code are copied, there is no loss in the quality of the copy and all the characteristics of the original file remain intact, as long as the copy process goes flawlessly. The copying process is also quite simple. A drag-and-drop procedure can be used to transfer a complete music album from the hard drive of a computer to a flash drive or a writable CD. Any standard personal computer can do the copy very quickly, so one is able to make a copy of a digitized three-minute song in less than 30 seconds. This ease in copying has led to the emergence of music piracy.

PIRACY OF DIGITAL SOUND

Music piracy is the term used to describe copyright infringement. As early as 1953, the *Stanford Law Review* described piracy as "the practice of re-recording a phonograph record manufactured by another company, and then selling the duplicates." Stealing music was relatively difficult in the age of the vinyl album, since the cost of manufacturing an album was too high for there to be a big business in selling duplicated albums. Once music began being released on cassette tapes, the process of piracy changed. Blank cassette tapes were readily available and it was relatively easy to make multiple recordings of a piece of music on them. The pirate would purchase one copy of the original music and thousands of blank cassettes on which to record the music. Then, pirates would sell the copies and keep the profits for themselves.

The band or musician who recorded the original cassette would gain nothing from the sale of the pirated cassettes, and the music industry would also fail to profit. When an original cassette or CD is sold in a legitimate store, part of the money paid for it goes to the company that helps to produce it, and a part goes to the artist or artists who create the music. Therefore, the producer and the artist lose their source of income if people do not buy the original cassettes or CDs, but instead settle for the cheaper copies.

The problem with music piracy in the era of the cassette was somewhat controlled by the fact that there was a noticeable loss in the quality of the music when it was copied from the original. Listeners who were interested in listening to the higher quality of the original recording would stay away from the cheaper and poorer quality copies. The problem with the quality reduction disappeared, however, with the development of better technology and the digitization of music. Now the copies sounded as good as the original. It was easy to record perfect copies of a CD, as long as the pirate could gain access to the original digital file, which was usually available on the CD released by the music company. The copying process would involve compressing the file into an mp3 format from the original format of the CD version, and then distributing that either by selling it through Web-based outlets or by producing new CDs from the mp3 files.

The digital music pirate is not the typical person who would have been involved in the illegal music trade in the days of the cassette. Digital piracy only requires access to a computer, a CD writer, and a connection to the Internet. Today, a high school student could easily create an mp3 file from a CD using a personal computer and software such as the Windows Media Player program that is provided free with any computer operating on the Windows system.

As mentioned in the case of Napster, after a person makes the mp3 file available to everyone in a peer-to-peer group, others on the network can copy the file at no cost. A personal music library can be increased by copying files from others on the network. By not paying for any of the music that is copied, all the members of the

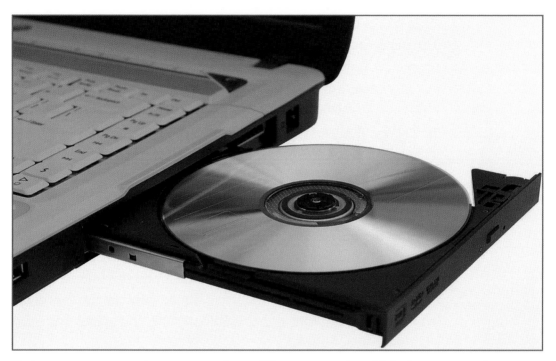

Today, most personal computers have CD programs in which the user can burn, or copy, data onto a CD. There is also CD burning software for computers without this program. According to the recording industry, individuals making their own music CDs have had a negative impact on sales of recorded music, resulting in a financial loss to the songwriter, the music company, and the merchants.

P2P network are considered to be stealing the music. Anyone willing to exchange digital music files is a music pirate, since he or she is bypassing the music industry to gain access to music.

Digitization of music essentially led to an explosion of music piracy, with every consumer being a potential pirate. According to the International Federation of the Phonographic Industry (IFPI), 20 billion songs were illegally downloaded in 2006. Based on that information, Stephen E. Siwek of the Institute of Policy Innovation reported in 2007 that "because of music piracy, the U.S. economy loses a total of $12.5 billion in economic output each year." Such staggering numbers have led to an urgent industry-wide examination of what needs to be done to stem music piracy.

PROTECTING RIGHTS

The music industry is made up of two major players and several supporting groups. The production of music begins as a creative act on the part of the musicians. Music companies invest large amounts of money in establishing professional recording studios, elaborate marketing mechanisms, and a large infrastructure that needs the flow of profit to operate. They also promote the work of a promising musician and eventually record his or her music and sell it in music stores. Ideally, the industry is able to sell the work of the musician to make a profit, which is shared among all the people involved in creating the music. The music industry survives on the profit that comes from the official sales of the music. Profits decrease due to music piracy. None of the money made from the sale of pirated music comes back to the industry. Those who are in the music industry want to protect their right to make the profit from the legitimate sale of music.

Piracy also violates the rights of those involved with the creative side of the industry. They, too, make a profit from the legitimate sale of music, but they have another important stake in the matter: the right to protect their creation from unauthorized use. Musicians put their intellectual and creative energy into making music, which becomes their intellectual property. Just like there are laws that protect the rights to tangible property, such as a house, there are laws that protect the intellectual property of those who create art. Piracy violates the intellectual property rights of musicians, and there are mechanisms to protect those rights as well. The laws that protect the music producer and the artists are called copyright laws. Digitization could violate the copyright laws.

TECHNOLOGIES FOR PROTECTING COPYRIGHT

The majority of music is legally distributed as uncompressed digital files that are lasered onto commercially produced CDs and sold through various distribution channels (such as music stores and online stores). As previously mentioned, a standard computer with a CD drive can burn the digital files off the CD to decode them and store them on the computer hard drive by using Windows Media Player. (Burning means to create your own custom CD using your computer.) The file can then be compressed into the mp3 format. This is called "ripping" music off the CD, and it produces a near-perfect copy of the original music. The copied file can then be used in many different ways: shared on the Internet, copied onto flash memory, or simply e-mailed to another person.

CD manufacturers have developed a method to protect their product against piracy by including a computer program on the CD that will not allow the ripping program to work. In such cases, the music files can be decoded only into analog sound that can be played through the computer speakers and the potential pirate would not be able to produce a digital copy of the original file. Technological protection has some disadvantages, since it also stops legitimate ripping of music, which has become a necessity with the explosion of personal digital music players. People who purchase a legal CD might want to make a copy for personal use on a portable digital player such as the iPod.

Copy protection technology does not allow any kind of ripping, which has led to the development of complicated copy protection software that would allow legitimate ripping while stopping the illegal ripping. The programs sometimes do not work very well and there is much customer dissatisfaction. The complicated copy protection software developed by Sony made computers vulnerable to unexpected technological problems. "Security experts said that anti-copying technology used by Sony BMG could be adapted by virus writers to hide malicious software on the hard drives of computers that have played one of the CDs," reported John Borland in 2005 on *CNET.com*. These problems make it difficult to apply the copy protection programs universally to all CDs.

It is also possible to write programs that disable copy protection software, allowing users to work around most of the copy protection software. There are many computer programmers who create these counter-programs and have made them available for downloading from the Internet. Some of these programs are commercially available through Web-based companies such as SlySoft. The company is based in the West Indies and it processes its payments through Ireland, making it difficult for U.S. authorities to stop its operation. The music industry is in a constant struggle to come up with better programs to protect the content of a CD. At the same time, there are programmers who are writing software to beat the industry efforts.

LEGAL PROVISIONS OF PROTECTING DIGITAL SOUND

Protecting music copyright by legal means is a complicated process because there needs to be a clear statement of whose rights are being protected, as well as what is being protected. There is quite a bit of confusion about how the laws would be written and what they would accomplish. For example, the RIAA wants to protect the rights of the musicians and the music industry, but there are some musicians who want to freely distribute their music over the Internet and not participate in universal copy protection legislation. In 2004 the Pew Internet and American Life Project released a report that claimed that artists were not deeply concerned with the file sharing that happens on the Internet.

In some cases, digital tools also make it easy for amateur musicians to distribute their music over the Internet. New musicians might not have the support and legal protection of the music industry, but they still hope to gain popularity by allowing free access to their music over the Internet. Such musicians might not be very supportive of legislation that outlaws the downloading of music. These different issues have caused tension among some musicians and the music industry. The laws that are created to protect music copyright need to take into account the changes that are happening

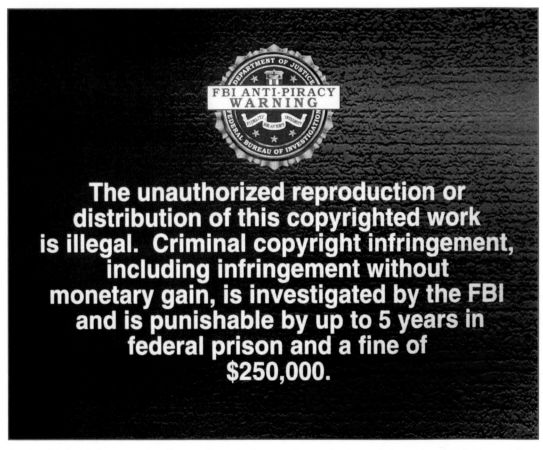

FBI ANTI-PIRACY WARNING

The unauthorized reproduction or distribution of this copyrighted work is illegal. Criminal copyright infringement, including infringement without monetary gain, is investigated by the FBI and is punishable by up to 5 years in federal prison and a fine of $250,000.

In the United States, the Recording Industry Association of America (RIAA) and the Federal Bureau of Investigation (FBI) have taken measures to combat digital piracy. Countermeasures include encrypted DVDs, software designed to crash and delete on pirated video games, and warning screens seen at the beginning of films and on CDs, such as the one shown above.

in the music industry. Authoring these laws becomes a complicated process because many different aspects of the industry need to be considered when thinking of legislative ways to control music piracy.

It is also important to remember that the Internet is a global medium; thus, piracy also is a global phenomenon. People use the Internet for global commerce to buy products from other countries

DIGITAL RIGHTS MANAGEMENT

The response of the music industry to the process of piracy has been the development of the tools for Digital Rights Management (DRM). The term DRM refers to the different ways in which the digital rights of the music industry are protected. One of the ways of doing DRM is producing CDs on which the digital rights are technologically managed. A system such as Extended Copy Protection (XCP), developed by Sony, is one way of doing DRM. There are problems with such methods, however. The Sony system came under significant attack since it installed a computer program on the hard drive of the user's computer without letting the user know about it. Many users who listen to music on the computer were upset by this. The users were so unhappy that, according to the technology correspondent for MSNBC, finally "Sony announced it would suspend production of CDs with the technology."

There are other systems, such as the one provided by the largest DRM company, Macrovision, which has been protecting media content since 1983, 15 years after the introduction of the prototype for the first widespread video cassette by Sony. The Macrovision system has become popular with the music industry since it does not make changes to the user's computer. This system places special computer programs on CDs, making them difficult to copy. The Macrovision system is not very effective, however, because users can easily find programs that crack the protection.

DRM technological methods have not been very successful, leading to the adoption of specific laws in the United States and the European

with just the click of a button. Computer programs like SlySoft are often sold by being directly downloaded from users in various countries, making it difficult to stop piracy since laws can only be enforced in the country where the laws were written. For example, copy protection laws that can be enforced in England might be

Union. In the United States, the law is called the Digital Millennium Copyright Act (DMCA). It was adopted in October 1998 and offers extensive legal protection to the creators and distributors of digital products. The law includes all different forms of digital information, including material such as computer software, which is also widely pirated across the globe. The DMCA is very broad in its statements and criminalizes all attempts to get around the anti-piracy efforts that are built into digital products. For example, legal action could be taken against someone attempting to undo the codes used by Macrovision.

One of the key issues in the DMCA is that it does keep open an allowance for people making copies for "fair use" of the material. The idea of "fair use" has been a troublesome part of copyright protection, since it is vague in terms of where copies may be made if the copier was able to demonstrate that there was an intent of fairly using the copy. This is a slippery statement because it allows pirates to use it if prosecuted under the laws of the DMCA. If fair use cannot be proved, courts in the United States can award up to $150,000 for every infringement of the DMCA.

In 2001 the European Parliament provided a set of DRM instructions called the European Union Copyright Directive (EUCD) to member countries. Any European country can enforce these laws, although only a few countries have actually made the EUCD into law. In Europe, each country follows its own copyright laws that have been upgraded to serve as DRM systems. In the end, the process of DRM needs to begin with the consumer of digital music. It is possible that DRM will occur quite naturally if legitimate music is available at a price that is affordable to all.

meaningless in Peru. This suggests that copyright protection laws should be enforced by multicountry agreements, in which similar laws are adopted universally. In actuality, this is a complicated issue because political relations between different countries might make it impossible for one country to support another's laws.

Another major problem regarding copyright protection laws is that they are meaningless unless they can be enforced. The police systems in different countries must be willing to work together to make sure the laws are indeed followed by everyone. The legal systems in different countries must agree that there will be adequate punishments when the laws are broken. This is difficult to achieve because the enforcement systems vary widely. In India, for example, the enforcement people might have been bought off with bribes by the pirate groups. In the United States, the enforcers might be overwhelmed if they attempt to prosecute every college student who is illegally downloading music. In either case, there are gaps in the process of enforcement and the laws become ineffective in regulating piracy.

Ultimately, the issue of piracy will have to be determined by the user. Only when the user decides not to purchase pirated music will there be a sizable decrease in the market. Then piracy will cease to be a profitable business. "The only way to prevent teenage girls from freely sharing boy-band mp3s will be to provide a service that's reasonably priced and irresistibly better than free file sharing," said Dan G. Wallach of Rice University in an article in *Computer Society* magazine during the early days of music piracy. "Any other technology, business model, or legal framework is simply doomed." That concept has yet to be developed, making pirated music a continuously profitable trade.

The Future of Digital Music

This volume has examined some of the key components of digital music and audio. Listening to music has been a popular activity for a long time and the development of sound digitization has allowed people to enjoy music in a way that is very different from earlier methods. Digitized audio has provided new ways of designing a lot of different tools. These developments could have significant social and cultural influences as digital audio is becoming a staple of contemporary culture.

The development of tools that combine different functions, including manipulation of digital audio, could change the way people listen to music. The rapid miniaturization of microprocessors, which also continue to become increasingly powerful, allows manufacturers to build in many different functions into one gadget. The iPhone is one of the best examples of such a tool. It allows the user to listen to music as well as do many other tasks such as take pictures and make phone calls. Such developments could

In 2007, Hewlett-Packard unveiled the HP TouchSmart at the International Consumer Electronics Show in Las Vegas, Nevada. The TouchSmart is the first mass market touchscreen desktop computer.

allow users to carry fewer gadgets and accomplish more with fewer tools.

These developments also include the development of "all-in-one" gadgets that could become more of an entertainment unit than a computer. These gadgets would look different and do much more than the personal computer. Such a gadget, called the HP TouchSmart, was developed by Hewlett-Packard in 2007. The TouchSmart, which is now in its fourth version as of 2009, was the first mass market touchscreen desktop personal computer. There is a touch sensitive monitor that connects to a computer that can hold thousands of songs and can also be connected to a cable television line. Other components include a webcam, Bluetooth, a Blu-ray drive and burner, and a TV tuner with remote. Such a unit merges the functions of the computer with a traditional music system or television and has already been shown in two hip-hop music videos (by the Black Eyed Peas and Scooter Smiff). Today, users relate to a computer no longer as just a work tool, but also as a tool for entertainment.

The notion of entertainment also changes since the digitization of technology allows listeners to customize their entertainment experience. These tools provide a great deal of control over the listening experience, so the listener is no longer dependent on the music that is packaged by the music industry. As Andrew Moylan comments in *The American*, "No longer are consumers forced to purchase entire albums to hear the one song they like." That situation is replaced by the downloading of music, with the music customers being able to select only the songs they want and then compile their own libraries. The age of shelves lined with thousands of CDs in a music store could be replaced by a single Web site with a search box that would allow the buyer to type in a specific name in order to pluck the music off the Internet. It is a process made possible not only by the digitization of music, but also by the increasing availability of connections to the Internet.

The relationship between the Internet and digital music is also the cause for some of the problems related to the way in which digital music is traded. The music industry will have to tackle the rampant illegal downloading of music from the Internet. The consumer is able to easily obtain music that can be illegally shared with others. The issue of digital rights management will become more complicated as the music industry gets more internally torn about how to deal with digital piracy and the tools to decrease it. Some segments of the industry are leaning away from enforcing DRM, as evidenced in 2008 by Sony's announcement to put its entire catalog of tracks on the Amazon mp3 store. Decisions such as this could become more common as the music industry realizes that there are fewer ways to control the way in which digital music is used.

The use of digital audio could also become more popular as digital sound is built into different appliances and machines. People would be able to use their voices as a way to interact with computers, making for a more natural way of interaction compared to the traditional keyboard and mouse. In some cases the voice-based interaction could actually make it safer and easier to operate tools. "One theme at CES [the 2008 Consumer Electronics Show] is the development of touch-screen and voice-activated controls for portable devices," reported the *Winston-Salem Journal.* "Cars are showing that off, too, with systems that let people make phone calls, navigate, choose music, and have e-mails read to them without dangerously fumbling for manual controls." Innovations such as this could significantly improve the quality of life for future generations.

Chronology

3100 B.C. Numbers with 10 base used in Egypt.

A.D. 628 Indian mathematician Brahmagupta suggests that zero was a real number and offers rules for its use.

1040 Printing press developed in China by the Chinese inventor Bi Sheng, who carved Chinese characters with wood.

1200 The abacus is used to do mathematical calculations in China.

1439 Johannes Gutenberg develops the printing press in Europe.

1666 The idea of the binary number system using zero and one is introduced.

1822 Charles Babbage designs the first mechanical computer, using the idea of binary numbers.

1876 Alexander Graham Bell patents the first telephone.

1904 John Fleming makes the vacuum tube that can be used as an electronic switch.

1923 Interpol established as an international police force to fight international crime.

1927 *The Jazz Singer* is released as the first movie to use sound.

1947 John Bardeen builds the transistor that replaces the vacuum tube.

1948	Howard Aiken develops an electronic computer with 5,000 vacuum tubes.
	Patent issued for Cathode Ray Tube Amusement Device, starting the era of digital games.
1953	IBM introduces the model 604 computer with transistors.
1956	IBM introduces the magnetic hard drive as a storage medium.
1957	IBM introduces the model 608 computer for the commercial market.
1964	John Kemeny and Thomas Kurtz develop the BASIC computer program language.
1967	The analog sound generator Moog synthesizer is adopted by rock band the Monkees.
1969	DARPA funds the development of an international network of computers.
	The lunar module lands on the moon, using a computer smaller in capacity than a personal computer of 2009.
1970	Digital Electronics Corporation introduces the personal dot matrix printer.
1975	Industrial Lights & Magic established by George Lucas to use computer graphics in making movies.
	Byte magazine is launched as the first magazine dealing with digital technology.
	The PLATO networked education system serves 146 locations in Illinois.
1977	Apple Corporation introduces the Apple II computer.
1978	Roy Trubshaw, a student at Essex University in the United Kingdom, starts working on a multiuser adventure game called *MUD* (*Multiuser Dungeon*).

1980   Polydor Company of Hanover, Germany, produces the commercially available compact disc.

Pac-Man game released in Japan.

1981   Microsoft develops the DOS computer program as the operating system for computers.

IBM introduces the first personal computer using the MS-DOS operating system.

1982   The Groupe Spécial Mobile (GSM) cell phone technology is developed by the Conference of European Posts and Telecommunications (CEPT).

The compact disc is introduced in the United States.

1985   Intel introduces the 80386 microprocessor, with 275,000 transistors built into the chip.

The computer program WELL is set up to allow a community of people to exchange computer files with one another.

The C++ computer language is released commercially.

1986   The Farooq Alvi brothers, operating out of Lahore, Pakistan, release the first computer virus called "The Brain."

1987   German scientist Dieter Seitzer develops the mp3 format for digitizing sound.

1989   The European Center for Particle Research (CERN) in Switzerland invents the World Wide Web.

SimCity developed as an alternative to shoot-up digital games.

Nintendo introduces the Game Boy in the United States.

1990   Commercially available digital still camera sold by Logitech.

Code Division Multiple Access (CDMA) cell phone technology is developed by Qualcomm.

1992 First Short Message Service (SMS) message sent from a cell phone.

1993 Intel introduces the Pentium microprocessor, with 3.1 million transistors built into the chip.

Researchers at the University of Illinois at Urbana-Champaign introduce Mosaic as a tool to browse data on the Web.

1995 *Toy Story* is produced by using only computer-generated images to create a complete movie.

Presidential Savings Bank is the first bank to provide the option of doing financial transactions on the computer.

Pierre Omidyar, a French-born Iranian computer scientist, establishes the prototype for the online auction Web site eBay.

1996 Health Insurance Portability and Accountability Act (HIPAA) is introduced, placing strict regulations about who may have access to the health information of Americans.

Palm introduces the personal digital assistant (PDA).

Travelocity.com launches an online system for selling airline tickets.

1997 The digital video disc (DVD) is introduced in the United States.

Movies begin to be released on DVDs.

TiVo is introduced to digitally capture television shows.

Instant Messaging (IM) technology is introduced by companies like America Online (AOL).

"Deep Blue" computer beats Garry Kasparov at chess.

1998   The United States adopts the Digital Millennium Copyright Act (DMCA), which offers extensive legal protection to the creators and distributors of digital products.

Printed version of *Byte* is discontinued after 23 years in publication, having been the first magazine to deal with digital technologies.

New Media & Society is launched by Sage Publications to examine the role of digital technologies in society.

The Motion Picture Experts Group standardizes the MP4 format for capturing and storing digital video.

Google begins with a $100,000 investment as a company operating from a garage.

2000   Nearly 5,000 satellites are in space.

Trek Technology and IBM introduce the flash memory as a storage medium.

Google becomes the most popular Internet search tool.

2001   Apple introduces the iPod.

Wikipedia is launched as a freely editable online encyclopedia.

2003   Linden Research Laboratories introduces Second Life as a multiuser social game.

United Nations Educational, Scientific and Cultural Organization (UNESCO) begins a special award on digital art through their "DigiArts" mission.

MySpace is introduced as a social networking Web site.

2004   Two-thirds of Americans claim to use instant messaging on a regular basis.

Liberated Syndication offers the first podcast hosting service for a $5 monthly fee.

Revenue from the sale of digital games doubles from the 1994 sales level.

The Food and Drug Administration (FDA) approves the use of an embedded microprocessor in the human body for medical purposes.

2005   Steve Chen, Chad Hurley, and Jawed Karim introduce YouTube.

In one of the largest breaches of the security of personal information, 40 million Visa and MasterCard credit card numbers become available to anyone on the Internet.

Ninety percent of all videos sold in China are illegally produced pirated copies of the original DVD.

Microsoft introduces the Xbox 360 game system.

In the United States, the number of identity thefts exceeds 250,000.

Google introduces Google Maps as a digital mapping tool.

2006   Eleven years after its launch, eBay has 200 million registered users worldwide.

Sony introduces the PlayStation3 game system.

Nintendo introduces the Wii game system.

Sun Microsystems releases Java as a computer program that anyone can freely use.

Facebook becomes available to anyone in the world.

In Britain, the number of surveillance cameras reaches 4.2 million, 1 for every 14 people.

On average, the number of spam e-mails sent per day reaches 12.4 billion.

2007   In a single month, more than 24 million users visit the YouTube Web site.

American consumers spend about $30 billion shopping on the Internet during the Christmas shopping season.

Sales of the LCD screen surpass sales of the CRT screen worldwide.

Apple introduces the iPhone.

James Cameron and Vince Pace develop the 3-D Fusion Camera System to shoot feature films in stereoscopic 3-D. It is used to shoot several films, including *Aliens of the Deep*, *The Adventures of Sharkboy and Lavagirl*, and *Ghosts of the Abyss*.

2008   The number of airline tickets sold on the Internet exceeds the number sold through travel agents and other offline systems.

2009   All television stations in the United States begin broadcasting digital signals.

2010   James Cameron's film *Avatar*, which is made almost entirely of computer-generated animation using the 3-D Fusion Camera System, breaks the record for highest-grossing film of all time. It is also the first movie ever to earn more than $2 billion worldwide.

Glossary

America Online (AOL)   A private company providing Internet access for a fee.

analog   A signal that delivers data continuously in time and amplitude; can be converted into a digital signal.

Apple Corporation   A private company manufacturing digital goods.

archive   A collection of historical records of information.

Atari   A private company manufacturing digital game products.

binary system   A system that represents numeric values using only two digits, usually zero and one.

Bose Corporation   A private company manufacturing audio systems like speakers.

British Broadcasting Corporation (BBC)   The state-owned radio and television broadcasting organization in Great Britain.

broadband   A method of sending digital information that allows a large amount of information to be sent in a short time.

buffer   A temporary space where digital information can be stored for a short period while the computer processes the information.

C++ language   A widely used computer programming language used in a large range of applications.

Center for Disease Control (CDC)   An American government agency that is concerned with the health and safety of people.

chat room   A type of computer program available on the Internet that allows several people to communicate with one another in real time.

compact disc (CD) A storage medium for music or computer data.

computation A specific mathematical operation, such as an addition or subtraction, performed by a digital tool like a cell phone.

computer code A series of letters and numbers that makes up the instructions given to a computer.

computer monitor A device that acts as the interface between the user and the computer, showing the texts and images produced by the computer.

computer program A series of commands given to a computer, instructing the computer to perform a series of tasks.

data storage system A way to permanently save large amounts of digital information.

digital A quantity, measurement, or signal represented by a series of discrete numbers; an analog signal can be converted into a digital one by sampling its value at periodic intervals.

digitize The process of converting a continuous quantity, having a numerical value at each instant, to a quantity represented by discrete numbers.

download A process of moving digital information from a centralized repository of data to a personal digital device like a personal computer.

electron An atomic particle having a negative charge; currents flowing in many conductors, such as metals, consist primarily of electrons in motion.

electronic bulletin board A computer program that allows group members to send information to a centralized computer so that all group members can access the information.

Entertainment Software Rating Board (ESRB) A self-regulatory American organization that calibrates entertainment products like computer games and other digital entertainment products based on suitability for different age groups.

fiber-optic line A cable that uses pulsating light to transmit digital information.

forum   A computer program that allows a group of people to exchange digital information by placing the information on a centralized computer accessible to all group members.

Game Boy   The trademark of a handheld digital device used for playing digital games.

handheld controller   A portable device, like a small remote control, that is used to control the operations of a digital device.

handheld game machine   A portable digital device that is used to play digital games.

hard drive   A device that is used in digital machines to store information.

high-speed connection   Same as BROADBAND, a method of sending digital information that allows a large amount of information to be sent in a short time.

intellectual property   A legal right of ownership over the creations of the mind, such as music, art, literature, and scientific ideas.

interactive   Describing a process in which every step of the process is dependent on the previous step, as in the case of a conversation in which each message is based on what was just said.

International Business Machine (IBM)   A multinational company that pioneered the manufacture of a computer for personal use.

Internet   The connection of numerous computers where each computer can interact with any other computer on the network.

Java   A special type of computer program that has become very popular for use with Web sites, because the programs can be interpreted by any kind of computer.

keyboard   A device that has a button for every letter of an alphabet and is used by computer users to interact with computers.

local area network (LAN)   A connection between computers that are spatially close to each other, as in the case of a set of computers in a private home.

Magnavox An American company specializing in the manufacture of home electronic products like televisions, radios, and DVD players.

memory A component in a digital device that is used to store information, both for long periods of time and short periods of time while the device does computations.

microprocessor A component in a digital device that contains microscopic electronic switches that are etched onto a tiny piece of silicon, making up the most important part of all digital devices.

Microsoft An American company that produces the Windows operating systems used in computers worldwide.

mouse A device used with a computer to simulate the movement of a pointer on the computer screen by moving the physical pointing device on a flat surface.

nationality The identity of a person based on a person's citizenship documents, such as passports.

networked A process that connects different digital devices with each other.

networked environment A working condition where many different digital devices are connected to one another.

Nintendo A Japanese company that manufactures and sells handheld computer games, devices, and digital game systems.

Nintendo DS A more advanced version of GAME BOY.

nodal computer A machine that makes up the center of a network of computers.

personal computer (PC) A machine that can be used by a single individual as a personal computer to perform many different digital tasks.

personal digital assistant (PDA)   A handheld digital device that keeps a record of contacts, appointments, tasks, and other personal information.

platform   The fundamental computer program, like WINDOWS, that provides the support for a large range of computer programs.

PlayStation   A personal digital gaming device created by Sony that has the characteristics of a personal computer and also contains a built-in high-definition DVD player.

process   A specific set of tasks that a digital device performs to provide a specific function like large statistical calculations.

refresh   The way in which the image on a COMPUTER MONITOR is periodically updated to reflect changes in information sent to the computer.

shooting games   A category of digital games that uses a replica of a gun or cannon to shoot at objects on the screen.

Sony   A Japanese company specializing in the manufacture of home electronic products such as computers, televisions, radios, and DVD players.

statistics   A special branch of mathematics focusing on creating estimates and trends by looking at a large amount of data about a specific phenomenon.

text-based message   A form of communication that uses only letters of the alphabet.

virtual   Any system or phenomenon that only exists as a digital file without any tangible component.

web-based magazine   A category of publications that does not have a paper version but exists only on the Internet.

Web   The short and colloquial term for the World Wide Web computer program that uses a universal computer language to exchange different kinds of digital information among computers connected to the Internet.

Wii A personal digital gaming created by Nintendo that uses wireless, motion-controlled remotes.

Xbox A personal digital gaming device created by Microsoft that has the characteristics of a personal computer and also contains a built-in high-definition DVD player.

Bibliography

Balzevic, J. "Upgrade Your PC: Audio." *PC Magazine,* March 16, 2005. Available online. URL: http://www.pcmag.com/article2/0,1759,1765344,00.asp.

Bartimo, J. "They May Not Be Technology's A-List, But . . . They've Changed Your Life." *PC Magazine*, September 4, 2001. Available online. URL: http://www.mywire.com/a/PCMagazine/They-May-Not-Be-Technologys/433996?page=2.

Bloomfield, M. W. and L. Newmark. *A Linguistic Introduction to the History of English.* 1st ed. New York: Alfred A. Knopf, 1963.

Borland, J. "Sony to patch copy-protected CD." *CNET.news,* November 2, 2005. Available online. URL: http://news.cnet.com/Sony-to-patch-copy-protected-CD/2100-7355_3-5928608.html.

Borland, J. "Chasing digital music's 'codec killers.'" *Cnet.news,* October 22, 2004. Available online. URL: http://news.cnet.com/Chasing-digital-musics-codec-killers/2100-1027_3-5414121.html.

Bull, M. *Sounding Out the City: Personal Stereos and the Management of Everyday Life.* New York: Oxford, 2000.

Carbone, J. "Hard-disk-drive price decline slows." *Purchasing* 136, no. 15 (December 2007).

Clukey T. "Capturing Your Sound: A Guide to Live Recording." *Music Educators Journal* 92, no. 3 (January 2006): 26–32.

Coulton, J. "What music format is the best?" *Popular Science*, January 22, 2006. Available online. URL: http://www.popsci.com/diy/article/2006-01/what-music-format-best.

Fries, B. and M. Fries. *Digital Audio Essentials.* O'Reilly Media: New York, 2005.

Geer, D. "Digital music faces incompatible formats." *Computer Publication* 39, no. 4 (April 2006): 10–12.

Kozinn, A. "Exotic Influences in High-Tech Concert." *New York Times*, June 5, 1988. Available online. URL: http://www.nytimes.com/1988/06/05/arts/reviews-music-exotic-influences-in-high-tech-concert.html.

Laing, D. "A Farewell to Vinyl?" *Popular Music* 11, no. 1 (January 1992): 109–110.

Lyman, J. "Apple-Microsoft Rivalry Renewed with Music Format Wars." *TechNewsWorld*, February 2, 2004. Available online. URL: http://www.technewsworld.com/story/32749.html.

Miller, M. "Playing Digital Music on Your Home Audio System." *InformIt*, November 18, 2004. Available online. URL: http://www.informit.com/articles/article.aspx?p=351419.

Miser, B. and T. Robertson. *iPod and iTunes Starter Kit.* 2nd ed. Toronto: Que (Pearson Technology Group Canada), 2005.

Moylan, A. "The End of Big Music?" *The American*, November 14, 2007. Available online. URL: http://www.american.com/archive/2007/november-11-07/the-end-of-big-music.

Musgrove, M. "A Messy Age for Music: Confusion Reigns In the Expanding Digital World." *Washington Post*: October 22, 2006. Available online. URL: http://www.washingtonpost.com/wp-dyn/content/article/2006/10/21/AR2006102100120.html. Accessed January 2, 2010.

Nieminen, J. "Computer-Based Music Production on a Budget." *Digital Web Magazine*, April 21, 2004. Available online. URL: http://www.digital-web.com/articles/computer_based_music_production_on_a_budget.

Schurman, K. "Digital Audio: Despite Compression & Copyright Concerns, The Beat Goes On." *Smart Computing*, November 2001. Available online. URL: http://www.smartcomputing.com/editorial/article.asp?article=articles%2Farchive%2Fg0911%2F33g11%2F33g11.asp&articleid=11148&guid=&searchtype=0&WordList=&bJumpTo=True.

Tommasini, A. "Hard to Be an Audiophile In an iPod World." *New York Times*, November 25, 2007. Available online. URL: http://www.nytimes.com/2007/11/25/arts/music/25tomm.html.

Wallach, D. S. "Copy Protection Technology is Doomed." *Computer Archive* 34, no. 10 (October 2001): 48–49.

Further Resources

Books

Berners-Lee, Tim. *Weaving the Web: The Original Design and Ultimate Destiny of the World Wide Web.* New York: HarperCollins, 2000.

Campbell-Kelly, Martin and William Aspray. *Computer: A History of the Information Machine.* New York: Westview Press, 2004.

Gates, Bill. *The Road Ahead.* New York: Penguin Books, 1995.

Gregg, John R. *Ones and Zeros: Understanding Boolean Algebra, Digital Circuits, and the Logic of Sets.* New York: Wiley & Sons–IEEE, 1998.

Hafner, Katie and Matthew Lyon. *Where Wizards Stay Up Late: The Origins of the Internet.* New York: Simon & Schuster, 1996.

Jenkins, Henry. *Convergence Culture: Where Old and New Media Collide.* New York: New York University Press, 2006.

———. *Fans, Bloggers, and Gamers: Media Consumers in a Digital Age.* New York: New York University Press, 2006.

Lessig, Lawrence. *Remix: Making Art and Commerce Thrive in the Hybrid Economy.* New York: Penguin Books, 2008.

Negroponte, Nicholas. *Being Digital.* New York: Knopf, 1995.

Nye, David E. *Technology Matters: Questions to Live With.* Cambridge: Massachusetts Institute of Technology Press, 2006.

Palfrey, John and Urs Gasser. *Born Digital: Understanding the First Generation of Digital Natives.* New York: Basic Books, 2008.

Schneier, Bruce. *Secrets and Lies: Digital Security in a Networked World.* New York: Wiley & Sons, 2000.

White, Ron and Tim Downs. *How Computers Work, 8th ed.* Indianapolis: Que Publishing, 2005.

Web Sites

Centers for Disease Control and Prevention

http://www.cdc.gov

A government-run Web site that has information related to effects of computer use on health.

Central Intelligence Agency

https://www.cia.gov/library/publications/the-world-factbook

Web site of the U.S. Government intelligence agency that provides information about digital crime all over the world. The CIA Factbook is also a good source of information about different places.

Entertainment Software Association (ESA)

http://www.theesa.com

U.S. association exclusively dedicated to serving the business and public affairs needs of companies that publish computer and video games for video game consoles, personal computers, and the Internet.

Exploratorium: The Museum of Science, Art and Human Perception

http://www.exploratorium.edu

An excellent web resource containing much information on the scientific explanations of everyday things.

Geek.com

http://www.geek.com

Resource for news and developments on all aspects of digital technology.

HighDef Forum

http://www.highdefforum.com

This Web-based forum offers information related to the developments in digital and high definition video.

HowStuffWorks, Inc.

http://www.howstuffworks.com

Contains a large number of articles, generally written by knowledgeable authors, explaining the science behind everything from computers to electromagnetism.

Institute of Electrical and Electronics Engineers

http://www.ieee.com

International organization involved in the study of computers.

International Communication Association

http://www.icahdq.org

The association offers Web-based resources to understand how human communication works in general and in the context of digital technologies.

Interpol Cybercrime Page

http://www.interpol.int/public/TechnologyCrime/Default.asp

Contains information on the efforts Interpol, an international police organization, is making to prevent digital crime in different regions.

Library of Congress

http://www.loc.gov/index.html

This excellent Web site is a resource for doing research on many different topics using digital technology.

Motion Picture Association of America

http://www.mpaa.org

This Web site offers information on how the different digital music and video formats have evolved and explores the current issues regarding digital video and music.

Psychology Matters

http://psychologymatters.apa.org

A Web site with information on the psychological aspects of computer use.

Science Daily
http://www.sciencedaily.com
*Links to information on the developments in basic science
research that have an impact on the development of digital
technologies.*

Picture Credits

Index

About the Author

Ananda Mitra, Ph.D. is the chair of the Department of Communication at Wake Forest University. He teaches courses on technology, popular culture, issues related to South Asia, and research methods. He has been a technology commentator for regional, national, and international media, such as *Time* magazine. Mitra has published articles in leading communications journals as well as two books.